MW01600609

THE POWER OF ONE

From the Ashes of Struggle to the
Seat of Superintendency

(The Unheard Journey of Dr. Michael D. Triplett)

ISBN- 979-8-218-64961-6
Printed and bound in the United States of America
First Printing 2025
Editing by Kimberli Wilson
Book cover design by Kennedy Davis
Interior formatting by Sierra Dean

To order additional copies of this book, contact the author:
Michael D. Triplett, Ph.D.
Email: miketrip1992@gmail.com
Website: www.triplesolutionsllc.com

This book will not only tell my personal story but will serve as a guide and inspiration for those who feel stuck, hopeless, or lost in their circumstances. Whether someone is battling poverty, struggling to find purpose, or seeking a path to leadership, this book is a testament that no situation is permanent and that one person, one decision, and one moment can change everything.

This is not just my story; it's a message to anyone who has faced adversity: You have the power to rise. You have the power to lead. You have the power to change your life.

Table of Contents

Dedication
To Those Who Poured into My Life

As I stand where I am today, it is not just the result of my own hard work, it is the combination of the love, guidance, and unwavering support of so many who poured into me, and lifted me when the world doubted me and left me in a horrible mental space.

First and foremost, I want to thank GOD for giving me the fortitude and strength to see beyond any dark situation. I know that it is because of my faith and belief in him that I am who I am today, unapologetically. To my wonderful mother, Zenobia C. Agnew (RIH), my siblings, Tommy, Chris, Carl, Poke Chop, Kim and Kita, *Ant Neely*, and my entire; Turner, Richardson, Hendricks, Wiley, Jackson, Williams, Hughes, and Triplett families, thank you. I would also like to thank my many Friends, Teachers, Coaches, Cafeteria Workers, Custodians, Bus Drivers, etc. You were my first teachers. You taught me what it meant to fight, push forward, and never let my circumstances define me. You led by example and taught me resilience, love, and the power of unwavering faith. When times were tough and the weight of the world pressed down, it was you who reminded me that I came from strength. Your sacrifices, your lessons and your love made me who I am.

To my East St. Louis community, my Masonic Brothers: You were my proving ground, my foundation, and my fire. This city, with all its challenges, also held limitless dreams. It taught me to be sharp, relentless, and to never let fear stop me from walking through doors that were meant to be mine. Every hardship I endured, every obstacle I overcame – I did not do alone; because East St. Louis breeds warriors, and I am proud to be one of them.

To Lane College: You gave me more than an education; you gave me a purpose, a family, and belief in what was possible. The students, staff, and entire campus climate, all played a part in developing the leader I have become. I am forever grateful to President Chambers, Dean Thomas, Dr. Garcia, Mr. & Mrs. Kirkendoll, Ms. Loveland, My East St. Fellas, The Ques (Kappa Sigma Chapter – Those Five Hounds From Hell; Delmos Cauley, Stanley Stubbs, Allen Lane, Eric Roberson and me of course). The Pearl's, My LC brothers and sisters, you saw something in me, nurtured it, and pushed me toward excellence; and you continue to do so even today.

As I reflect on my professional journey: Every role I have held, from teacher, social worker, assistant principal, principal, and program director in St. Louis Public Schools; assistant superintendent in Riverview Gardens School District; assistant and associate superintendent in Olathe School District; to current superintendent in Normandy School District; was more than just a title. It was a mission. It was an opportunity to serve, uplift and fight for change.

To every mentor, colleague, and leader who challenged me, guided me, or simply gave me a chance--thank you. Your lessons, advice, and even your criticism, helped to shape me into the leader I am today.

And finally, to my students: You are the reason I tell my story, the fire that keeps me pushing forward, the source of my refusal to give up, the motivation needed as I fought to sit at decision-making tables and my catalyst to continue advocating for change. Why? Because I see myself in you. I know your struggle. I know the weight of carrying dreams while the world tells you they are impossible. But I stand before you as living proof that you can make it, you can rise, you can achieve anything you set your mind to.

If you remember nothing else, remember this: Your past does not define you. Your circumstances do not limit you. Your struggles do not break you; they build you. Like me, you too, can write your story. You are powerful. You are capable. You are destined for greatness. So, to all who have poured into my life, know this-- your investment in me was not in vain. I carry your wisdom, your love, and your legacy with me in everything I do. Know this my students, I see you. I believe in you. And I will never stop fighting for you.

THE POWER OF ONE
From the Ashes of Struggle to the Seat of
Superintendency
(The Unheard Journey of Dr. Michael D. Triplett)

A Journey from the Streets to Superintendency

East St. Louis wasn't just where I grew up, it was where I was forged. The city, known more for its struggles than its victories, was both my battlefield and my proving ground. It's where I learned the meaning of survival long before I ever understood the concept of success. It's where I first encountered hunger, not just for food, but for a life beyond the limits of my circumstances. And most of all, it's where I first grasped the idea that sometimes, it only takes one decision, one belief, or one opportunity to alter the course of a life.

This book is not just my story, it is a testimony to the power of one.

Growing up in the 1970s and '80s, I saw the streets swallow people, whole kids who never got the chance to dream; mothers who fought to keep their children fed and fathers who disappeared into the system, never to return. I was born into a world of violence, gang wars, and drug-ridden neighborhoods where the sound of gunshots at night was as familiar as the sound of crickets in more quiet towns. The walls of our home weren't thick enough to keep out the chaos, and my mother's hardworking hands weren't enough to shield us from the cold realities of poverty.

By the age of four, I had already smoked my first joint, not out of rebellion, but because in our world, innocence didn't last long. By five, I understood that hunger wasn't just about food, it was about the way desperation could shape a person's decisions. By seven, I knew what it meant to fight, not for pride, but for survival. Yes, we were broke, the kind of broke where food was never guaranteed, where dinner might be a stack of dry pancakes with no butter or syrup, or a very big can of string beans passed around as breakfast. Clothes weren't bought; they were handed down, and by the time they reached me, they didn't fit. My baby brother and I tied rope around our waists to hold up oversized pants and cuffed them so many times they barely resembled the jeans they were meant to be. We made games out of nothing; playing Red Light, Green Light in the backyard, running through abandoned houses, throwing bricks at each other for fun because what else was there to do? The streets were our playground, but they were also our predators. We learned early that every step we took outside was a gamble.

Why Does This Story Matter?

This book is for every kid who grew up feeling like the world was set against them. For every mother who worked herself to the bone just to keep the lights on, and for every young man who has ever wondered if he would live past the age of eighteen. It's for those who have seen the inside of a juvenile detention center and thought it was the beginning of the end. For those who had to hustle just to eat and who had to fight just to walk home safely. The love from family, the protection from friends and when someone believes and pours into you, dreams become visions and visions become realities. But more than that, this book is for the ones who believe or need to believe that change is possible.

This book is not just about one person making it out. It's about the idea that one decision, one opportunity, one belief in something greater can shift an entire life's trajectory. I was supposed to be another statistic. The streets tried to claim me. Hunger tried to break me. The system tried to erase me. But somewhere along the way, I made one choice after another that led me not just away from the dangers of my youth, but toward a destiny that no one, not even I, saw coming. From a boy wearing too-big clothes and smelling like kerosene, to a man walking into boardrooms as a Superintendent, an Author, a Leader-- my journey is proof that the power of one is real. One voice can speak life into a struggling child / One opportunity can change a family's future / One belief in yourself can write your entire story.

Although this book is my story, it also serves as encouragement to the reader; that hope, resilience, and transformation is possible, no matter where you start. This book is about "The Power Of One".

FORWARD

In the eyes of Dr. Michael D. Triplett, I see the weight of a thousand struggles, the scars of hunger, the echoes of empty nights and the silent prayers of a boy who refused to be broken. His eyes carry the pain of a childhood where dreams felt like a luxury and survival was the only certainty.

Betrayal and letdowns, the moments when the world said, "You won't make it," the times when doors slammed shut, when hope felt like a flickering light in a storm of doubt. But within that storm, you also see an unbreakable will, a fire that could not be extinguished.

Love and sacrifice, the quiet resilience of a mother who stretched every dollar, who held her family together with prayers and perseverance. You see the unwavering loyalty to the students who walk the same path he once did, who look to him as proof that they too can rise.

Compassion, not just for the ones who believe, but for those who have given up, the young men who feel invisible, forgotten, discarded by a world that never expected them to succeed. He sees them, because he was them.

Hard work, grit, relentless determination and long nights spent in books while others gave in, to the streets, early mornings stepping into classrooms where he would teach, guide, and transform lives. You see the calloused hands of a builder, a warrior, a game-changer who never stopped fighting for a better future.

And in the depths of his gaze, beyond the battles fought and the mountains climbed, you see triumph, not just for himself, but for every student who dares to dream, for every young Black boy who needs proof that poverty is not destiny, for every doubter who said "you can't," and for every child who now believes "I can." You see a king, not because of where he sits today, but because of the journey it took to get here.

From Poverty to Educational Leadership – *An Inspiration for All*

A Childhood Marked by Struggle

His journey is not just one of success, it is one of survival, resilience, and relentless determination. Born in East St. Louis, Illinois, a city often synonymous with poverty, crime, and lack of opportunity, he grew up in one of the most impoverished areas in America. Life was never easy. He was the fourth of seven children, raised by a single mother who worked tirelessly just to put food on the table. There were nights when the family went to bed hungry, days when electricity or water was cut off, and moments when the weight of poverty seemed unbearable. Yet, despite these struggles, he refused to let his environment define his future. He saw the suffering, the limitations, and the despair around him, but he believed that education was his only escape.

Overcoming the Odds

The streets of East St. Louis were unforgiving. Drugs, violence, and crime claimed the futures of many young Black men around him. It would have been easy for him to fall into the same cycle that consumed so many in his neighborhood. But he chose a different path. Education became his salvation even when schools were underfunded and resources were scarce, he committed himself to learning. Mentorship was his anchor, he found guidance in teachers, family members, and community leaders who saw his potential and encouraged him to keep pushing forward. Faith and determination carried him through; even when society expected failure, he believed in his ability to rise above. There were countless obstacles: walking to school in worn-out shoes, struggling to study in a house with no heat, and watching friends fall victim to the streets. But no matter how tough things got, he refused to give up.

Breaking Barriers in Education

Despite the odds, he earned his degree from Lane College, an HBCU that shaped his growth and strengthened his commitment to uplifting others. It was there that he discovered his passion for education not just as a tool for himself, but as a weapon to break generational poverty for others like him. After college, he didn't stop. He knew that Black students, especially Black male students needed someone who understood their struggles, someone who had lived through their pain. His career as an educator became his mission. He implemented programs that focused on empowering young Black men, providing opportunities for success, and breaking cycles of failure.

Leading by Example

Today, he serves as Superintendent of Normandy Schools Collaborative, back in the St. Louis area where his journey began. He is not just a leader, he is living proof that no matter how difficult life gets, success is possible. From having nothing to leading entire school districts. From poverty and struggle to mentoring thousands of students. From being counted out to becoming a national voice for educational equity. His book, "Different Thinking Leads to Different Outcomes", provides a blueprint for educators and students on how to rise above adversity and achieve greatness.

A Message to Those Who Feel Hopeless

To every young person reading this who feels like life is stacked against them, Dr. Triplett is proof that YOU CAN

MAKE IT. It doesn't matter if you're growing up in poverty. It doesn't matter if you don't have role models around you. It doesn't matter if people doubt you. What matters is your mindset, your determination, and your belief in your own success. If Dr. Triplett can rise from extreme impoverished conditions, fight against the odds, and achieve his dreams, so can you.

Thank you, Dr. Michael D. Triplett, for being a beacon of inspiration for many.

INTRODUCTION

East St. Louis didn't just steal dreams, it made sure you never even thought about them. It didn't give you room to imagine a future because survival took up all the space. You didn't daydream about possibilities; you focused on what was right in front of you. And if you did let your mind drift to the future, the images were dull, jobs that paid the bills but never sparked excitement, a life built on making ends meet rather than making something of yourself.

I didn't spend a lot of time thinking about what I wanted to be when I grew up. That kind of thinking felt like a privilege; one I didn't have. But in sixth grade, for the first time, I started to give it some thought, not in some deep life-planning way, but in the simple sense of knowing what I didn't want to do.

I thought there was no way in hell I was going to be a teacher. Not a chance. Not after what I put my teachers through. I was that kid, the one who made teachers question their career choices, the one who turned lesson plans into survival exercises. I turned pop quizzes into debates, I saw substitute teachers as prey, and I figured out exactly how far I could push before getting kicked out of class. And I pushed "hella" hard.

Teacher? Uhhhhh, no, thank you. That job looked miserable. Standing up there day after day trying to make kids like me care about... prepositions and polynomials? Holding it together while some knucklehead in the back of the room cracked jokes, passed notes, and did everything but listen. That wasn't going to be me. I wasn't signing up for that kind of slow torture.

I had other thoughts. Big time thoughts. I wanted to be a fireman. Not just any fireman, but the one behind the wheel of those massive yellow trucks (back then in East St., they were yellow) with sirens blaring, tires screeching, smoke thick in the air. I wanted to be the hero bursting through flames, saving lives and making headlines. I sometimes dreamt of charging into burning buildings, my uniform soiled yet my determination, unshaken. The city would chant my name. Kids would point at me and say, there goes Michael Triplett, "the baddest firefighter ever."

It was the perfect plan. Firemen were cool. Firemen were heroes. Firemen didn't have to grade papers, deal with disrespectful kids, or worry about lesson plans. They got to break down doors, wield axes, and drive trucks that looked like something out of a superhero movie. Most importantly, nobody ever threw a spitball at a firefighter.

But life, as it always does, had other plans. Growing up the way I did, college wasn't something I saw in my future. It wasn't that I didn't believe in education or that I lacked the ability to succeed academically, but the idea of college felt distant, almost foreign. In my world, survival came first. The concept of planning a career, choosing a profession, or mapping out a future seemed abstract when the immediate reality was just making it through the day. I didn't know what I wanted to be or do because, in many ways, I had never been given the space to dream beyond what was right in front of me.

My understanding of work was shaped by what I saw in my home and in my community, people grinding to make ends meet, doing whatever it took to keep food on the table and the lights on. The word "career" wasn't something we used. People had jobs. They worked hard, not because they loved what they did, but because they had no other choice. Stability wasn't a goal; it was a luxury.

When you grow up in an environment where struggle is constant, your focus narrows. You learn to operate in survival mode. You think about how to get through today, not how to build a future for tomorrow. Dreams don't seem practical when you're worried about whether your family will have enough to get by. College felt like something meant for other people, for those who had the privilege of seeing past their circumstances.

I didn't lack intelligence, but I lacked exposure. I didn't lack ambition, but I lacked direction. Without guidance, without someone to show me what was possible, I simply didn't know there was more out there for me. I had never seen someone take a path that led to a profession, much less a fulfilling one. And when you don't see it, it's hard to believe it's real.

Somewhere along the way, the kid who swore he'd never stand at the front of a classroom; ended up doing just that. Not just standing there, but teaching, leading and inspiring. Maybe my teachers weren't suffering in vain. Maybe they weren't just dealing with me, but shaping me. Maybe, despite my best efforts to be a menace, they saw something in me that I didn't see in myself.

And maybe, just maybe, the biggest fire that was meant for me to fight wasn't the kind that needed a hose. It was the kind that needed a lesson, a conversation, and a chance to change someone's life.

A conversation that sparked a book about JUST who Dr. Michael D. Triplett is. I am not a celebrity. I am not an internet sensation with millions of followers hanging onto my every word. There are no flashing lights or paparazzi tracking my every move. My name doesn't trend on social media, and I have never been the face of a viral movement. Yet, I have walked through fire, climbed out of the depths of struggle, and risen to heights many never thought I would reach, not even I. I did not inherit success, I built it with my bare hands, laying brick by brick with the sweat of perseverance and the mortar of resilience.

Mine is not a story of golden opportunities or smooth transitions; it is a story of war. A war against obstacles, a war against doubters, a war against a world that told me I was not enough and a war against a city that craved struggles. I have faced resistance at every level, not because I was incapable, but because I dared to rise. Haters have lined my path like spectators at a coliseum, cheering for my downfall, gossiping about things they do not understand, and defaming my name before ever shaking my hand. But nothing, no rumors, no lies, and no unfair criticisms could have prepared me for what happened that day in Walgreens.

It was supposed to be a simple stop, just another moment in an ordinary day. But as I stood in the aisle, flipping through items on the shelf, I overheard a conversation unfolding a few steps away.

"That no-good superintendent in Normandy, always dogging people out, trying to take credit for everything happening there," a woman spat out, her voice filled with a kind of certainty that suggested she had personally witnessed my every decision. I paused, feeling the weight of her words settle in the air around me. There was no anger, just a deep, knowing exhale. I had lived this before; assumptions and baseless accusations. People who had never walked in my shoes decided they knew my journey better than I did. But that day, I decided to engage.

"How do you know him?" I asked, turning toward her. She didn't hesitate. "Oh, I know him well. Worked in a previous district where he was. I had to go off on him a few times." She said it with pride, as if she had confronted some villain and emerged victorious. I tilted my head, curiously. "Have you ever thought about making an appointment to talk to him? To sit down, face-to-face, and have a real conversation?" She scoffed. "That would be a waste of time. He's an irrational mo-fo (you know what I mean)."

The weight of irony hung between us like an invisible anvil. She spoke with such certainty about a man she had never even met, and yet, she claimed he was the one unwilling to listen. I took a breath, steady and composed, then asked, "What's your name?" She hesitated, as if suddenly realizing she had entered dangerous waters. Then, in an instant, she flipped the question. "Well, what's yours?" I looked her in the eyes, my voice calm but unwavering. "I am Dr. Michael D. Triplett." Silence...

The shift in her expression was immediate and undeniable. Her posture deflated, her bravado evaporated, and for the first time, I saw something beyond baseless assumptions and embarrassment. She stood there, realizing in real time that she had just spoken ill of a man she had never met, never worked with, never truly known. And in that moment, I understood something deeper about my journey. My battle has never just been against systemic obstacles or professional challenges. It has also been against ignorance, against narratives people speak and have written about me before they have even taken the time to understand the man behind the title or the name.

I was not supposed to be here. A kid from East St. Louis, forged in the fires of struggle, should not have made it to the superintendent's office. But I did. Not because I was given anything, but because I fought for everything. And no matter how many people doubted me, no matter how many rumors had been told, no matter how many critics whispered in the aisles of drugstores, one thing remains true: I am still standing. This is my story and mine alone to tell. SO BUCKLE UP! ! !

Chapter 1

THE STREETS THAT RAISED ME

East St. Louis: *A City That Can Make or Break You*

East St. Louis isn't just a city, it's a battlefield. A place where childhood is something you survive rather than something you enjoy. Where the streets don't just teach you lessons; they test you. And if you fail, they don't give you a second chance. The air itself carried the weight of the struggle. It smelled like desperation in the summer, when heat waves turned the cracked pavement into a furnace, and the tension in the streets rose with the temperature. It smelled like gunpowder in the fall, when the nights grew longer, and somebody's mother was bound to get that dreaded knock on the door. The winter? That was the season of hunger. Of barely making it. Of stretching everything, food, heat and hope until it was threadbare.

There were neighborhoods in East St. Louis where stepping outside the wrong house at the wrong time could get you killed. And it wasn't just gangbangers and street hustlers who had to worry. The violence didn't discriminate. It didn't care if you were a good kid just trying to get to school. Bullets had no conscience. They had no GPS trackers. They traveled wherever anger, revenge, and chaos sent them. By the time I was old enough to understand the world around me, I already knew that fear was a luxury I couldn't afford. Being scared got you tested. Got you marked. Got you caught slipping. I learned early that looking too long at the wrong person, in the wrong place, could be seen as disrespect. I learned that survival didn't just mean staying out of trouble, it meant knowing when to speak, when to disappear, and when to fight back.

RAISED BY THE STREETS

Growing up in East St. Louis wasn't just about learning how to live, it was about learning how not to die. It was normal to hear gunshots before going to bed, to wake up to news of another body found in an alley, another life swallowed by the city. We didn't flinch when we heard sirens. We didn't react when the streetlights flickered over abandoned houses that had become trap spots. We walked past the addicts with hollow eyes and the neighborhood alligators with blood on their hands like they were part of the scenery because in a way, they were. I didn't just live in East St. Louis; I was raised by it. And the city didn't raise its children gently. It toughened them. Hardened them. Bent them until they either broke or became unrecognizable. I watched boys I played with in elementary school turn into ghosts lost to the system, lost to the bullets, lost to the streets. Some of them didn't even make it to middle school, let alone high school. The city had a way of turning soft hearts into stone. It made good kids cruel. It made innocent eyes go dark. It made survival the only thing that mattered. For a long time, I thought danger was normal. I felt comfortable around chaos because it was all I had ever known. I remember walking to school and passing a group of men huddled around a dice game, the smell of weed and liquor mixing with the early morning air. I remember watching fights break out over debts that would never be paid, watching men disappear into alleyways with desperation in their eyes and guns on their hips. I remember knowing, even as a boy, that this city didn't just chew people up; it swallowed them whole. And the worst part-- It dared you to think you were different.

THE CITY THAT BREAKS SOULS

East St. Louis didn't just claim bodies. It claimed souls. It turned laughter into silence. It turned hope into something you stopped believing in. The weight of the struggle, the generational pain, the systemic neglect and the hardening of people. I saw men who had once dreamed of something bigger give up. I saw women who had fought for their families lose their battles to addiction, to exhaustion, to a world that refused to give them a break. The schools were underfunded. The jobs were scarce. The resources were damn near nonexistent. It was a city where the system failed you before you even had a chance to prove yourself. The world looked at East St. Louis and saw a war zone. But for those of us who grew up there, it was home. And that was the hardest part, it truly meant loving a place that was trying to devour you.

THE FIGHT TO ESCAPE

I had every reason to become another statistic and every opportunity to let the streets claim me. From moment to moment I could have made a choice that would have led me down the same road as so many before me. But something inside me wouldn't let me go (totally). Maybe it was my family, the ones who refused to let me slip. Maybe it was the teachers and mentors who saw something in me that I hadn't yet discovered in myself. Maybe it was the nights I lay awake, staring at the ceiling, promising myself that I would not die here. Leaving East St. Louis didn't mean forgetting where I came from. It meant proving that survival was possible and that escaping the cycle wasn't just a dream, it was necessary. The city tried to raise me for the worse.

East St. Louis wasn't just a city. It was a battlefield, a lesson, a trap, and a hustle all rolled into one. If you weren't tough, both mentally and physically, you would struggle tremendously to make it. If you didn't have a certain level of street savviness or as we would call it, "game," you got swallowed whole. And if you were poor…Man, you had to fight for every damn thing, every single day. I was born into the struggle. Ain't no sugarcoating that. My mom was busting her ass as a nurse's aide, getting paid under the table barely making pennies. Seven kids, one woman, and a house that always seemed to be missing something: food, heat, electricity, etc. Pick a struggle, we had it. Our house wasn't a home, it was a survival zone. Winters? Freezing. Central heat? Damn, back then we didn't even know such a thing existed. What we had was a kerosene heater that sat in the middle of the room, filling the air with that sharp, throat-burning smell. That smell seeped into all our clothing, skin, and hair. At school, kids used to clown me, saying I smelled like "Kerosene 33," a combination of kerosene and Brut 33. It stung at first, but I learned quickly that either you let people laugh at you, or you learned how to "Jone" back. I got good at it. Really good. No one was about to out-roast me. And oh, by the way, there is nothing like getting kicked out of your first school at the age of seven for beating your baby brother up over a girl. Not that I wanted her but because he told me that I had better not touch her. So, I did, and I dusted him. Full disclosure, that was probably my twentieth time getting in trouble, so my principal at Cannady at the time Boo-jack (Mr. John Bailey Jr.) expelled me. You see, I was the Dennis The Menace of Cannady Elementary School.

MY DNA - MOMMA, GRANDMA AND DADDY

My mother Zenobia C. Agnew (RIH) was the type of woman legends are made of, a force of nature who refused to let life's hardships define her or her family. She was tenacious, resilient, and unyielding. The kind of woman who could stare down adversity and bend it to her will. No matter how little we had, she made sure we never felt like we were missing anything. She had a way of creating magic out of thin air, transforming the mundane into moments we would later learn to cherish forever.

Her stern presence commanded respect. She didn't play games when it came to the serious stuff; school, respect, and integrity were non-negotiable in her house. A bad report card or a disrespectful word to an adult would ignite her wrath, and trust me, you didn't want to see that side of her. But that sternness wasn't just discipline; it was love. She demanded excellence because she saw it in us, even when we couldn't see it ourselves. She refused to let the world break us because she knew how unforgiving it could be.

When holidays rolled around, my mother became a miracle worker. We didn't have much, sometimes we didn't have anything, but you'd never know it. For Christmas, she would find a way to get a tree, even if it meant pulling one from the side of the road and brushing it off like it was fresh from the store. She'd somehow get gifts, no matter how small, and wrap them with care, turning our modest living room into wonderland. On birthdays, she'd bake cakes from scratch or improvise with what little we had, and her smile made us feel like we were royalty. She had this uncanny ability to make us feel seen, wanted, and celebrated, even when the world outside our door didn't.

But she wasn't all firm and grit, my mother had a fun-loving side that lit up our world. She could tell a joke, sing a song, or dance around the kitchen like she didn't have a care in the world. On Friday nights, she'd gather us with her homemade popcorn, and we'd laugh and bond as though we were the richest family on the block. She had a laugh that could fill a room and a spirit that could lift even the heaviest hearts.

Yet beneath that warmth was an unshakable strength. My mother was a problem solver, a fixer, a creator of possibilities, an Olivia Pope (from the series Scandal). If the lights went out, she'd light candles and turn it into an adventure. If we didn't have enough food, she'd stretch every meal with the skill of a chef, making it taste like a feast. When times got tough, which was often--she held us together, never letting us see her crack under pressure. She bore the weight of the world on her shoulders, and somehow, still had the energy to remind us of how much we mattered to her.

She was our anchor, our guide, and our greatest cheerleader. She showed us what love looked like; unwavering, sacrificial, and fierce. Even when the odds were stacked against her, she found a way to make us feel safe, important, and loved. My mother was and still is, a testament to the power of resilience, the strength of a mother's love, and the ability to create beauty in the face of struggle. She didn't just raise us; she shaped us, molded us, and gave us the tools to stand tall in a world that often tried to knock us down. To us, she wasn't just a mother; she was a HERO.

My grandmother Lille Mae Richardson (RIH) was the cornerstone of our family, a woman whose tough love shaped us in ways we didn't always appreciate at the time but can never forget. She was as steady as a rock, a woman of few words but deep wisdom, who believed in discipline, hard work, and the power of tradition. Her methods were strict, no doubt, but they were also rooted in love, the kind that teaches you not just to survive but to thrive. She was a true protector and played no games.

Her house was like a boot camp for life. She had no problem assigning chores, and everyone pulled their weight. Cooking and cleaning weren't optional; they were part of the routine. She made sure we all knew how to cook, no matter how young we were, and took turns washing dishes like clockwork, weeks at a time. If a holiday fell in your week, you didn't just help, you ran the show. That meant preparing the meals, setting the table, and scrubbing every dish until it sparkled. It was a rite of passage, and though we grumbled, we learned responsibility and pride in our work.

Holidays were sacred in her home, and she made sure we felt their significance, even when times were lean. Christmas was particularly special. She would assemble "Goody Bags" for each of us, filled with the simplest treasures, nuts, apples, oranges, tangerines, pears, and quite a bit of candy. It may not sound like much, but to us, it was everything. That was the only time we got to indulge in sweets, and those bags felt like gold. She knew how to make something so small feel monumental, and it taught us to cherish what we had, no matter how little it was. On a side note, I think Grandma had a little scratch, she just didn't let us know.

Church was non-negotiable. Every Sunday she made sure we were there, dressed in our best, whether we wanted to be or not. I remember one Easter, we had on corduroy suits; skipping wasn't an option, and she saw to it that we understood the value of faith and community. Church wasn't just about religion; it was about discipline, knowing there was something bigger than ourselves, and about learning to respect time-honored traditions.

Her tough love could be intimidating, but it was never without purpose. When she corrected you, it wasn't to belittle you but to make you better. She held us to high standards because she knew the world outside her home wouldn't cut us any slack. She prepared us for life's challenges by teaching us to be accountable, to work hard, and to never expect anything to be handed to us.

My grandmother wasn't the type to coddle, but she showed her love in ways that left a lasting impact. She made sure we knew how to fend for ourselves, care for a home, and cook meals that brought the family together. She didn't just raise us, she trained us, shaped us, and instilled in us a sense of duty, resilience, and gratitude.

Looking back, I see that her tough love was a gift. She didn't just teach us how to cook or clean, she taught us how to be resourceful, how to show up even when we didn't feel like it, and how to appreciate the small joys in life, like a Christmas Goody Bag or a home-cooked meal. My grandmother's love wasn't soft, but it was fierce, unyielding, and utterly transformative. She was the quiet architect of our strength, and everything she did was for our benefit, even if we didn't realize it at the time.

My father's love, Carl F. Hendricks (RIH) was different; a quiet, steadfast presence that shaped me in ways I only came to fully understand as I grew older. He wasn't the type to coddle or shower you with constant affection, but his expectations were clear, his lessons firm, and his love unmistakable. His was the kind of love that pushed me out of my comfort zone and taught me to stand on my own two feet.

He believed in the power of hustle and earning your place in the world through hard work and determination. From a young age, he made it clear that nothing worth having would be handed to me. He expected me to go out and get it for myself. "If you want it, you have to work for it," he'd say, and he meant it. He taught me the value of a strong work ethic, not just by his words but by his actions. He was a living example of what it meant to persevere and to never rely on anyone else to do for you what you could do for yourself.

But my father's lessons didn't stop at hustle; he also taught me the importance of relationships. He was adamant that life was as much about the bridges you build as it was about the obstacles you overcome. "Never burn bridges," he'd warn, "because you never know when you'll need to cross them again." He instilled in me the importance of respect, integrity, and leaving a positive impression on others. He showed me how to build connections, maintain them, and use them to create opportunities not just for myself; but for those around me.

My father's love wasn't loud or overbearing, but it was constant and purposeful. He pushed me to dream big and never allowed me to wallow in excuses. If I failed, he'd make me reflect, learn, and try again. He didn't just want me to succeed; he wanted me to understand what success required; grit, resilience, and the ability to see the bigger picture.

There was an unspoken strength in the way he loved me. He believed in me, even when I doubted myself, and his confidence became the foundation for my own confidence. His love taught me to value independence, cherish relationships, and to take responsibility for my future. He gave me the tools to navigate life's challenges and the wisdom to understand that no success is achieved in isolation. My father's love was the quiet wind at my back, steady and unrelenting, always pushing me forward, teaching me to be both self-reliant and connected to others.

FAMILY FEUDS: *The Art of Sibling Warfare*

Growing up with six siblings in a house where space was limited, food was scarce, and tempers flared faster than a matchstick in the wind, fights weren't just common, they were daily rituals. In our house, you had to be tough, not just because the streets required it, but because your own brothers and sisters were your first battleground. We weren't just any set of brothers. We were gladiators. Tommy and Kita, my oldest brother and youngest sister were the gentle ones. I don't know how they made it in this household. Plus, Kita was the household snitch protected by Tommy because he had Momma and Grandmom's ears. The sibling's love was a stone-cold trip.

CHILD NUMBER ONE:

Tommy – ***The Rescuer****: The one who threw one too many*

We were warriors, strategists and survivors. At least, that's what we told ourselves. In reality, we were just a bunch of reckless kids with no business playing the most dangerous game of war ever invented, hurling bricks at each other like we were medieval soldiers defending a castle. It was war in its purest form. There were no alliances, no safe zones, and no mercy. If you weren't fast, you were a target. And if you weren't accurate, you were in trouble, because retaliation was always coming. We ducked, dodged, and launched bricks with all the precision our young arms could muster. No helmets. No shields. Just raw instinct and the kind of foolish bravery only kids have.

Nonetheless, in our world of chaos, there was one person above it all, Tommy. Tommy wasn't like the rest of us. While we were crammed in the basement, surviving off whatever scraps we could find, Tommy lived upstairs. That was a whole different realm. Upstairs meant warmth, food, and other resources that were not available to us who lived in the basement. It meant peace. It meant security. And Tommy, oh, Tommy was Grandma's favorite. He and our cousin Chucky could do no wrong in her eyes. That favoritism got them perks we could only dream of.

However, to give him credit, Tommy wasn't selfish. He was our rescuer. When Grandma rationed food like we were in a Great Depression reenactment, Tommy would sneak us extra scraps late at night. That boy moved like a ninja, slipping food into our hands like some underground railroad conductor for the hungry. No matter what, he made sure we ate.

But even rescuers make mistakes. And Tommy's came in the form of a well-aimed brick. It was one of our usual battles. The sun was hot, the ground was dusty, and the air was thick with tension. Bricks were flying like bullets. I had just bent down to pick up a rock when—BAM! A brick smacked me smack dab in my right eye. Everything went black for a second. Then the pain hit. Blood gushed down my face like in a horror movie. I stumbled back, holding my eye, knowing instantly that this wasn't just a little scrape. Tommy was at my side in seconds, but not out of concern, oh no. He had damage control on his mind. "Listen," he whispered urgently, looking around to make sure no one else had seen. "Tell Mom and Dad that Chris did it." I was barely standing, vision blurred, and all I could think was, Yeah, that sounds right. Chris. Poor, unsuspecting Chris. He was about to take the fall for something he didn't even see coming. And me? I was about to get off scot-free. So, I went home, clutching my bloody face, and told the biggest lie of my childhood: Chris did it. The moment those words left my mouth; Chris' fate was sealed. My dad wasted no time. He tore into Chris like he was trying to solve a problem with sheer force. Chris didn't even have time to explain. One minute he was minding his business, the next he was getting his butt tore out the frame. And you know what? I didn't feel bad. Not one bit. My eye was swollen, but I had no heat on me.

Tommy got away with murder, and I was an accomplice. But Chris? Oh, Chris never forgot. To this day, if you bring it up, he turns into a Doberman, ears twitching, eyes dark; he still holds that grudge, and I can't blame him. Tommy, our beloved rescuer, may have fed us, but he also played the game better than all of us. And that brick? Well, that was just another battle scar in the war we called childhood play.

CHILD NUMBER TWO:
Chris – *The Slasher: A whirlwind of problems*

My second-oldest brother? Now, he was something entirely different. Chris was the kind of danger that made the air in a room feel thinner. He wasn't loud in many cases. He didn't make threats. He didn't need to. His reputation did all the talking. Everyone knew Chris would cut you. And I don't mean in the metaphorical watch-your-back kind of way. I mean literally. He didn't fight fair; hell, he didn't fight at all. Fighting suggested there was some kind of back-and-forth, some kind of exchange. Chris didn't exchange blows. He ended things before they had the chance to begin. If you crossed him, you weren't going to get a second chance. And yet, in my infinite foolishness, I broke the second unspoken law of survival: Don't. Fool. With. Chris.

I don't even remember what I did, probably something small, something stupid. But the moment I realized my mistake, it was already too late. Chris didn't need to announce what was coming. He just moved. One second I was standing there, thinking I had a fighting chance. The next? My world detonated. He didn't just hit me, he descended on me like a damn hurricane. A blur of fists, an unstoppable force, striking from angles that should've been physically impossible. I swear on everything I love, I have never in my life stood face to face with someone and been hit from behind at the same damn time. Seven hundred and eighteen times. Okay, maybe not literally, but it sure as hell felt like that. A relentless, merciless storm, a rhythm of punishment that left me dazed, humbled, and educated. Because when it was over, I didn't just learn a lesson I lived it. That day, I understood something deep in my bones: Chris wasn't the kind of man you tested. Not unless you had a death wish.

CHILD NUMBER THREE:
Lloyd (Carl) – *The Fighter: The kid who giveth and taketh away*

Lloyd wasn't just a big brother he was a force of nature. Every family has that one sibling who seems to be built differently, like they were born with a steel frame and a don't-mess-with-me aura. That was Lloyd. He wasn't just tough; he was THE TOUGH ONE. The kind of dude who walked into a room and made people straighten up without saying a word. A former gangbanger, yeah, but more than that…he was the unshakable pillar of our family, the one you did not cross unless you had a death wish. And me? Well, I had a moment of absolute, undeniable stupidity. Maybe it was a teenage ego. Maybe I had watched one too many action movies. Maybe I was just feeling myself that day. But for some ridiculous reason, I thought I was ready to challenge Lloyd. Yeah, Lloyd. The one who never flinched. The one who could drop a man twice his size without breaking a sweat. I must've thought my time had come, that somehow, overnight, I had leveled up in the big leagues.

I was dead wrong. I squared up, fists clenched, ready to prove I was more than just the little brother who used to run behind him in the streets. I wanted him to see me as an equal. But before I even got a proper swing in—BOOM. The dude hit me square in the forehead. Not a warning tap. Not a playful jab. A full-fledged, grown-man punch. At first, I thought, damn, that was solid. Then I reached up to touch my forehead and felt something that should not have been there. My skin was stretching, swelling, a whole damn unicorn horn was growing out of my head. I looked in the mirror, and there it was, my transformation from regular kid to magical creature.

I barely had time to comprehend my new mythical status before—BOOM. A second hit. And just like that, the unicorn was gone. I didn't need a third lesson. I didn't need another round. Hello, I didn't even need an apology. What I needed was distance. So, I did what any intelligent person with an ounce of survival instinct would do, I left Lloyd the hell alone. And I kept that same energy for the rest of our childhood.

CHILD NUMBER FOUR:
Michael/Me (Mouse-Face, Mike, Shorty) – *The Menace of the Hood*

I was born into war. Not the kind fought on distant battlefields, but the kind waged in the streets, in the basement where we slept, in the very walls of our house where every day felt like another mission just to survive. Some people are raised normal, in my eyes. I came up with my fists clenched, my mind sharp, and my instincts honed like a blade.

I fought. A lot. Fighting wasn't a choice; it was a necessity. If you didn't fight, you got trampled. If you didn't stand up for yourself, you became a target. I wasn't about to be anybody's victim. Whether it was defending myself from kids who thought they could punk me, standing up for my siblings, or just throwing hands because the world felt like it needed a reminder that I wasn't to be messed with, I fought. And oh did I stay in trouble for it.

Punishment? That was my second home. I spent so much time grounded I practically had real estate in the concept. It didn't matter where I was, what I was doing, or even if I was guilty, if something went down, my name was in the mix. If a window got busted, that was me. If food went missing, it must've been me. If somebody cried? Guess who was getting blamed? I became the scapegoat, the one always in the hot seat, the one they kept trying to beat sense into --but the truth was I already had more sense than most people gave me credit for. Because while they were punishing me, I was out here surviving.

Yes, I was a thief, but not in a cynical sense. I stole, not for greed, but for survival. Food didn't just appear on our plates. Sometimes, the only way to make sure my family had something to eat was to take it. And I was slick about it. I didn't just sneak around; I moved like a phantom in the night, slipping in and out of stores, kitchens, anywhere that had something we needed. I had a mission: make sure we ate, no matter what it took. I snuck out of the house like it was my second job. When the walls started feeling too tight, when the hunger gnawed too hard, when trouble was brewing in the air, I was gone. Slipping through windows, sneaking down alleys, disappearing into the city like I belonged to the streets themselves.

But I wasn't just some reckless outlaw. I was a protector. Always. I watched over people, over things, over the ones who couldn't protect themselves. My siblings, my friends, even strangers who had no idea the fights I fought just to keep them safe. I never let someone suffer alone if I could help it. If I called you family, if you were a part of my world, I'd take the hits for you. That was just how I was built.

And then, there were the animals. Dogs, alley cats, anything with claws, teeth, or the same survival instincts I had. I understood them, and they understood me. I brought stray dogs and cats home like they were reinforcements, warriors meant to take back the basement from the army of sewer rats that had claimed it. Those rats had gotten bold, thinking they ran the place. But I had a strategy. I unleashed my feline soldiers, and let me tell you, it was a massacre. The rats didn't stand a chance. It was as if even then, I was assembling armies, leading forces, making moves that suggest I was always meant for something bigger.

In hindsight, despite all the fights, all the punishments, all the times I was counted out or thrown into the fire; I was never just some kid running wild. I was training. Every struggle, every battle, every stolen meal and every bruised knuckle was just another step toward something greater.

Some people are born into comfort, with opportunities laid out before them like a feast. I was born in the trenches, where the only way out was through sheer force of will. And you know what? I wouldn't change a damn thing. Because I think-- no, I know, I was destined for greatness.

The Fourth Born but first with a Curl, a Gold Tooth, and a Child.

I wasn't just the fourth born, I was the blueprint. The one who took the first punches life threw, the one who had to figure it out before anyone else. That came with a lot, responsibility, expectation, and hardship. But it also came with style. That curl? Legendary. I wore it like a crown. It wasn't just a hairstyle; it was a statement. It said, Yeah, I've been through it, but I still look damn good doing it. That gold tooth? That was proof I had stories. You don't get a gold tooth for nothing. You earn that. It was a badge of honor, a little bit of shine in a world that tried to dull me down.

And the child? That was the moment I knew it wasn't just about me anymore. See, when you're out in these streets, running, fighting, surviving, it's easy to think you're untouchable. But having a child? That changes everything. Because suddenly, it's not just about you making it, it's about making sure they do too. I had already been a protector my whole life, looking out for my siblings, my people, even the damn alley cats. But now? Now I had someone who depended on me in a way no one ever had before. It made me think differently. Move different. Fight smarter.

The streets didn't care that I had a kid or that I was still just a young man figuring it out. But I cared. And that's what set me apart. I wasn't going to be another statistic; another product of my environment who let the world break him down. I had already fought too hard to lose now. That's why, through it all, I knew destiny wasn't just calling me; it had been waiting for me.

CHILD NUMBER FIVE:
Darold (Pork Chop) – *The Dipper: My Childhood Nemesis*

And then there was my younger brother, Pork Chop (a former gang-banger). See, he was nicknamed because when he was one or two, he climbed on the kitchen table and ate hot ass porkchops with no teeth. Mom cooked them for dinner and this dude, with only gums-- ate all of them. Pork Chop was the sneaky one.

That boy could steal from Fort Knox if he wanted to. If something of mine went missing, I didn't even have to ask who took it. I already knew. I'd be getting dressed for school, looking for my shirt, my jeans, my damn socks—gone. I'd be losing my mind searching the whole house, knowing I just put them in my drawer the night before. Then, out of the corner of my eye, I'd see my younger brother sneaking out the damn window, MY CLOTHES on his back, running like he was escaping Alcatraz. He was fast too. No matter how quick I chased him down, by the time I caught up, he had already switched outfits with one of his friends, so I couldn't even prove it was mine. But when I got home, I beat him down.

Believe it or not, that wasn't even the wildest thing that ever happened between us. One day, we got into it over something, who knows what. Maybe he stole my clothes again, maybe I "joned" on him too hard or maybe we were just bored. But out of nowhere, this boy picks up a pair of scissors and chucks them at me. I ain't eve have time to move. **THWACK.** Next thing I know, the damn scissors are sticking out of my thigh. We both just stood there for a second, stunned. He looked at me. I looked at him. Then, the pain hit. I yanked the scissors out-- and my first instinct. Revenge. I wasn't about to just let that slide. So, I grabbed the first thing I saw, a para-knife and without thinking, I threw it right back at him. **THWACK.** Right in the chest. For a moment, I thought I had killed him. He gasped, clutched his chest, and I just stood there, frozen. But then, this boy looked down, saw the knife sticking out, and kept on talking crap like nothing happened. Chop could take whippings like Denzel Washington in the movie Glory. He was built for pain. Pork Chop and I through our many differences, became "ROAD-DOGS", he was/is my dude.

CHILD NUMBER SIX:
Kim – *The Silent Killer: Corn-curl and her wrath*

Kim was the smart mouth of the group. She did this for two reasons; one because she was protected, we knew not to put our hands on our sisters, and two, Kim was no chump.

Now, my sister Kim (the oldest of the two girls) wasn't one to play with either. I might've been scrappy with my brothers, but I knew better than crossing Kim. She had zero patience for my nonsense. One day, I must've done something to piss her off, probably got too big for my britches or said something slick. Next thing I knew, she was coming for me. Now, Kim didn't throw hands like my brothers. Kim threw objects. And this time? It was a whole damn can of corn. She chunked that thing at my head with the accuracy of a major league pitcher. I ducked, thinking I had outsmarted her, but the problem was, I had a curl. A whole damn Jheri curl. I had just washed my hair so you know I had to put extra activator in it to make it soft and shiny. That corn landed right in the middle of my curl and stuck. Then somehow, she began biting my leg. I was able to break loose from her choppers. I ran to the bathroom trying to shake it loose, but my hair had a damn grip on it. That corn wasn't coming out. Took me forever to get that corn out of my curls, and the whole time, Kim was in the next room laughing her ass off. I wanted to go beat her down, but when I looked, she had another can of corn in her hand.

CHILD NUMBER SEVEN:
Kita – *The Informant: A Smokin' Lesson We'd Never Forget*

Growing up in East St. Louis, we were no strangers to adventure or mischief. Kita, though? She was our biggest problem. That girl could snitch on a man whispering in a hurricane. If you so much as thought about doing something wrong, somehow, she knew, and next thing you knew, the whole world did too.

Now, this particular time, we had outdone ourselves. Menard Penitentiary was having a picnic, an actual picnic at a prison. Don't ask how we ended up there, just know we did. And as kids with a little too much curiosity and not enough sense, we swiped a pack of cigarettes (Marlboro) from a table when no one was looking. It felt like we had just pulled off the greatest heist of all time. We were ready to smoke like the grown folks.

Back at home, we hid the cigarettes in the ceiling of the basement, like it was buried treasure, and we knew that the Informant couldn't find them. At night, we'd sneak outside, light up, and choke our way through each cigarette, pretending we were cool.

Everything was smooth until Kita snitched. It must have been no more than an hour after our last smoke session when we heard Grandma's voice, that voice that made your soul leave your body before she even got to you. "Y'all wanna smoke, huh? Alright then, let's smoke." We knew we were doomed. She lined us up like prisoners of war, sat herself down on her bench at the table, and told us to light up. We hesitated. "Did I stutter?" Grandma barked. Hands shaking, we lit the cigarettes. One cigarette turned into two, then three. We thought it was over when the pack ran out, until she turned to my oldest brother Tommy. "Go to the store, get more."

At that moment, we knew. We had entered a different kind of suffering. Kim, poor Kim, started lighting her next cigarette using the butt of the last one like she was in some kind of smoke marathon. Grandma was like oh, damn, you are a pro. I swear the air was so thick you could have cut it with a butter knife. Then Grandma, she had the nerve to start chanting,

"Cigarettes, cigarettes, I'm gonna get more cigarettes," like she was in some twisted version of that old Kibbles 'n Bits commercial.

Then there was Chop. Oh, poor Chop. That boy got so dizzy he just sat there, eyes half open, looking like he had seen the other side. And because we were ridiculous, we started stuffing cigarettes up his nose like we were decorating a Christmas tree. He didn't even protest, just sat there, too far gone to care.

As for me? I was sick. I couldn't even sneak out of the house to go to practice. Football? Done. I didn't even want to see a pigskin after that. For a whole week, everything I ate tasted like an ashtray. It was like my taste buds had been permanently baptized in nicotine.

To this day, Kim and I won't touch a cigarette. The trauma runs too deep. But Chop? Well, that's another story. Some people never learn. And Kita? Oh, she got hers in due time. But that's a story for another day.

More Battles From Within.

A HOUSE FULL OF HUNGER AND PESTS

Man, we were "broke broke". Food wasn't guaranteed or at least, "traditional food," but when it did come, it wasn't what people would call a meal. Some nights, we ate dry pancakes, no syrup, no butter, just stacks of flour and water cooked in a skillet. Other days, we had nothing but string beans for breakfast. I ain't talking about with rice or meat, just straight-up string beans out the can, cold sometimes, 'cause we ain't have gas to cook. Hunger was normal. Our stomachs growling was just background noise to life. We weren't just sharing food; we was sharing clothes, too. The boys in the house rotated outfits like a damn uniform service. Five pairs of jeans, four brothers, figure it out. My baby brother and I? Man, our pants were way too big hand-me-downs from brothers that were way older, way bigger and I had REAL big brothers. But we had a system. We'd take some old rope, loop it through the belt holes, and tie it tight around our waists just to keep 'em from falling. Then we'd cuff 'em once, twice, three, four times, until we could at least walk without tripping over ourselves. Shoes? That was a whole different situation. We ain't have no brand names, no Nike, no Adidas, only three and four striped buddies. We had whatever we could find, and sometimes, that meant sharing those too. Have you ever had to switch shoes with your brother because his fit a little better for the school day? Yeah, that was real life.

Living in my grandmother's basement wasn't just rough, it was a constant fight for survival. It wasn't one of those cozy, finished basements with carpet and furniture. No, this was the kind of basement where the walls sweated in the summer, and the cold in the winter made you feel like you were sleeping inside a deep freezer. The kind where you learned really quick that you weren't the only ones who lived there, so did the roaches and the "Borats," our nickname for the rats that were so big they could've applied for a dog license. These weren't ordinary rats. These things moved like they paid rent. Bold. Unbothered. Some of them were the size of a chihuahua, and I swear they looked me in the eye like they were daring me to challenge their authority. And truth be told, they ran that basement. If we left food out, it wasn't ours anymore, it was a "Borats" buffet. Many nights, they ate better than we did. You'd wake up, go for a slice of bread, only to find out it had already been claimed. There were holes chewed right through the plastic and crumbs scattered like a crime scene. I remember one night, lying in bed, exhausted from the day, trying to ignore the sound of little feet scurrying across the floor. Just as I started to drift off, I felt something brush against my foot. My soul nearly left my body. I kicked so hard I almost knocked myself off the bed. I flicked on the light and caught one of those "Borats" mid-stride just sitting there, staring at me like, What? You got a problem? Man, I had a problem alright. The worst part wasn't just seeing them, it was knowing they were always there, even when you didn't see them. You'd hear them in the walls, scratching, chewing, plotting. Some nights, it felt like a full-on rat convention was happening inside the house. The roaches weren't much better. Those things were fearless. You couldn't even eat a meal in peace. One time, I sat down to eat a bowl of cereal, turned my head for two seconds, and when I looked back, boom, one was chilling right on the rim of my bowl like he was about to take a swim. I lost my appetite, really quick. It was a daily battle, us versus them. But no matter how bad it got, we had to make do. The world outside didn't care about our struggle. School didn't stop just because I spent the night fighting off rodents. Life kept moving, and I had to move with it. Looking back, that basement taught me something. It taught me resilience. It taught me that even when you're at the bottom, you can still find a way up. It taught me that circumstances don't define you, how you respond to them does. So yeah, I grew up in a basement where the "Borats" and roaches outnumbered us. But I refused to let that be my whole story. I was meant for more than just surviving. I was going to make it out.

Sunday service at my uncle's church was always entertaining to me, folks speaking in tongues, jumping around, catching the Holy Ghost like it was on sale. One particular Sunday, I decided to join in. Eyes closed, arms flailing, mumbling whatever came to mind. At first, it felt kind of fun, but after a while, I started getting tired. I cracked one eye open to see if the spirit had let everyone else go, but nope they were still going strong. The longest service ever. By the time we got home, I was drained, but dinner was waiting. As we sat around the table, my grandmother, never one to miss anything, asked, "How was church?" Before I could even answer, Kita blurted out, "Michael caught the Holy Ghost!" Without missing a beat, my grandmother scoffed, "That boy ain't catch nothing. He faked it." Just when I thought we were done, Kita chimed in again, "Grandma, I caught half the Holy Ghost today, and I'm gonna catch the rest next Sunday." A dead silence infiltrated the room. All of us froze, forks suspended in mid-air, staring at Kita like she had just committed a federal offense. We knew better than to play with Grandma and the Lord at the same time. I couldn't hold it in any longer I let out the wildest laugh, thinking maybe, just maybe, I could break the tension. Bad idea. Before I could even finish, **THWACK** Grandma's crutch caught me across the arm. Dinner continued in silence. Lesson learned.

SURVIVAL OF THE FITTEST

Looking back, our house was more like a boot camp than a home. It wasn't just about eating and sleeping, it was about survival. We loved each other, but we fought like we were training for a damn prison riot. But through all the battles, all the sneak attacks, all the bricks, knives, and corn, we made it. Lloyd taught me to respect my limits. My second-oldest brother taught me that some fights just weren't worth it. My younger brother taught me to lock my damn drawers at night. And Kim? Well, she taught me that you don't mess with a woman when she's mad, especially if she got canned goods nearby. Tommy and Kita didn't teach me jack. In fact, until the day my mother passed, Kita was still the house informant. You see, we weren't just siblings. We were warriors in training. And trust me, by the time the streets came knocking, we were already battle-tested. Why? Because that's how we survived. The only ones you could truly count on were the same ones who had just punched you in the face an hour ago. That's why. Because we were built for battle before we even knew what war was.

THE STREETS AIN'T GOT NO MERCY

East St. Louis in the '70s and '80s? Man, it was war. The kind of place where walking out your door could mean never coming back. The streets weren't just dangerous, they were hungry, and they fed on kids like me. Gangs ran everything. Every block had a crew, and every corner had somebody claiming something. If you didn't belong, you best walk with your head down and move fast. High school games? Man, they weren't just about basketball or football. They were warzones. By the time I hit junior high at Rock, I had already learned how to move. Don't look soft. Don't act scared. Don't trust nobody. I was fighting all the time, not because I wanted to, but because I had to. If somebody tested you, you swung first. If you didn't, they would come back every day, trying you until you broke. And once they knew you were weak-- It was over. After every single junior high and high school game, we knew a fight was coming. Somebody was getting jumped, somebody was getting shot, and somebody was getting caught slipping. Many times, after games, we were on our bus headed back to our side of town and were ambushed. We couldn't even make it three blocks before another school's crew started throwing bricks at our bus. Windows shattered, kids screaming, glass flying everywhere, that wasn't anything new, though. That was just what happened. You survived or you didn't, but you bragged about the experience the next school day.

THE HUSTLE AIN'T JUST A GAME, IT'S SURVIVAL

With no money at home, my brothers and I had to figure something out. This is when I learned the art of hustling. It started with little stuff; collecting Pepsi bottles and redeeming them at Nationals (a chain of grocery stores in the St. Louis Metro area) for a dime. But that wasn't enough so, I got creative. My brothers and I go to the grocery stores, find carts full of groceries that old ladies and other folk couldn't carry, and offer to push their bags home for a couple dollars. Some paid, some didn't. But when you're hungry, you don't wait for a "yes" or "no." You just do what you gotta do. Then came the real hustling, stealing. Not because I wanted to, but because hunger doesn't care about morals. I learned how to swipe food from stores, how to grab and go, how to keep my hands quick and my face unreadable. I wasn't proud of it, but pride doesn't fill empty stomachs. By high school, I was deep in it. The streets had me, and I had no reason to fight against it. When you grow up in a place where violence is the norm and going to a friend's funeral is just another Saturday, you stop dreaming about a way out. You just start surviving.

NOT EVERYTHING WAS HARD FOR ME

I want you to know that my childhood wasn't just about struggle, it was full of laughter, creativity, and plenty of fun. We may not have had much, but we knew how to make the most of what we did have. On Friday nights, my mom always made sure to scrape together enough money for a bag of un-popped popcorn. She'd pop it freshly, pour it into a big brown paper bag, and we'd all gather at the foot of her bed to watch shows like; Hot Hit Videos, Putting On The Hits, The Benny Hill Show, Prison Cell Block H, Chillers' Theater, The Last

Picture Show and many more. Those moments were pure joy, simple but magical.

Saturday nights were our time to push boundaries, especially when Mom worked overnight. That's when we'd sneak in scary tv shows like Chillers' Theatre, movies like; The Blob, Phantasm, Halloween, and Friday the 13th. One time, we were watching Tarantulas, and I couldn't resist running my fingers up my sisters' backs. They screamed so loud my grandmother instantly knew it was me. She called my name with authority, "Michael!" and when I ran upstairs to explain, she punished me by making me spend the night in the dark, scary garage. It was 1a.m., pitch black, and terrifying. But did I learn my lesson? Of course not. Mischief was in my blood.

My grandmother had her own unique methods of keeping us in line. If my brother and I got into a fight, she'd make us whip each other. I can't count how many times we stood there, half-angry, half-laughing, trading weak slaps until she shouted, "Do it right, or I'll do it for you!" And whenever she summoned us, she had a flair for the dramatics. She'd stomp on the floor or bang her cane so hard; we'd argue over whose turn it was to go. "It's your turn! I went last time!" we'd whisper, but if we took too long, she'd call my name. She always called my name.

It wasn't all mischief and discipline, our days were filled with pure, unfiltered fun. The empty field next to our house became our baseball diamond. The milk crates we nailed to telephone poles became basketball hoops. We played Simon Says, Hide-and-Seek, Red Light, Green Light, It Tag, and Kickball. We raced in the streets and played sandlot football until the streetlights flickered on, a signal to head home or at least stay in the yard, but only in the back because, for whatever reason, we were prohibited from going on the front and the sides. On weekends, we'd get a little more freedom, stretching our adventures as far as we could before the 10p.m. bath-time call.

Some of the best times were our homemade Gong Shows. Mom was the judge, and although my little sisters always seemed to win, my little brother and I stole the show with our performances. We memorized songs and acted out skits, always competing to outdo each other. Even when we lost, Mom would make us keep performing because, secretly, she loved our antics. We were born entertainers.

Those are fond memories, I realize those days weren't defined by what we didn't have, but by how much we made of what we did. We turned brown paper bags into popcorn bowls, backyards into stadiums, and living rooms into stages. Life wasn't always easy, but it was rich with joy, creativity, and love. That's what truly shaped us.

A MINDSET MOLDED: *A Little History*

Walking through the streets of East St. Louis wasn't just a part of my daily life, it was a test of resilience, a lesson in survival I didn't fully understand until much later. The streets were more than cracked sidewalks and abandoned buildings; they were marked with stories of those who had fought battles and lost. Death was a constant companion, not in a dramatic sense, but in a way that seeped into the cracks of everyday life. It was in the memorials, candles flickering in the wind, teddy bears propped up against telephone poles and in the stories whispered on the stoop.

I remember Darnell, a kid I used to watch at the basketball court. He was a neighborhood star with a jump shot that seemed destined to take him far beyond the city limits. But one night, the court was quiet, except for murmurs about how Darnell had been gunned down over a pair of sneakers. Just like that, he was gone. I didn't cry, didn't even feel angry. I simply nodded when I heard the news, as if this was just the way things were. That numbness protected me, but it also scared me. Shouldn't I have felt something? But in East St. Louis, feeling too much could break you. The streets taught me that survival wasn't just about physical strength, but emotional control. To keep going, I had to build walls so high that nothing; fear, grief, or despair could climb over them.

There was one winter night that I'll never forget, a moment when East St. Louis truly put me to the test. I was around 15, walking home after basketball practice. The streetlights were dim, flickering like they could go out at any second, and the cold wind cut through my jacket. I'd taken this route home hundreds of times, but that night was different. I heard footsteps behind me, steady and deliberate. I didn't panic; East St. Louis taught you that panic made you a target; but my senses were on fire.

I turned a corner and saw a shadow break from the alley ahead of me. Two guys. They didn't say a word at first; they didn't have to. The look in their eyes told me everything. This wasn't going to be a conversation, they wanted something, and they were going to take it. I could've run, but something told me that wasn't the move. Instead, I stopped, met their gaze, and stood taller than I'd ever felt in my life. "You really want this to go down right here, right now?" I asked, my voice steady despite the knot in my stomach. They looked at each other, probably surprised I hadn't bolted. I took a step forward, narrowing the gap between us. "Because if you're gonna do it, you better be ready for what comes next." My bluff was thin as paper, but in that moment, it didn't matter. Confidence, real or not was my armor. One of them chuckled, shrugged, and muttered, "Not worth it." They turned and walked away like nothing had happened. But something happened. I learned that night that sometimes, the fight is over before it starts if you know how to carry yourself.

Another time, I learned that not every battle ends clean. I was 12, and there was a bully in the neighborhood who made it his mission to terrorize anyone smaller than he, which included me. For weeks, he'd shove me into walls, snatch my backpack, or throw my shoes into the street. I told myself to let it slide, but the day he ripped a book out of my hand and tossed it into a puddle, I snapped. I waited for him after school, hiding behind a fence near the bus stop. When he passed, I stepped out and shoved him as hard as I could. He stumbled, more shocked than hurt, and turned to come at me. But this time, I wasn't backing down. The fight wasn't long or pretty, but it ended with him on the ground and me standing over him. I didn't feel triumphant, just relieved. After that, he left me alone. That fight taught me that sometimes, you must make a stand, even if it costs you. And then there were the quiet lessons, the ones no one else saw. Like the nights I sat on the front steps of our building, watching people argue, hustle, and dream. I realized that in East St. Louis, everyone was fighting something: poverty, prejudice, addiction, or even themselves. The difference between those who made it and those who didn't, wasn't just strength, it was how they fought. The ones who survived knew when to push, when to pivot, and when to let go.

East St. Louis didn't just shape me; it forged me. The city was harsh, but it was honest. It taught me to stand tall, choose my battles wisely, and never, ever underestimate the power of resilience and strategy. Every scar, every story, every lesson is etched into who I am today. The streets didn't stop teaching though. One night, I was walking home through a neighborhood I knew too well. I heard footsteps behind me, steady and deliberate. My body should have screamed at me to run, to panic, to get out of there. But I didn't. I turned the corner, straightened my posture, and walked forward, steady and unbothered. Fear had no place in me anymore. It wasn't bravado, it was survival. That night, nothing happened. The footsteps eventually faded away, and I made it home. But it hit me later: my lack of fear, my numbness, wasn't just protecting me, it was defining me.

And then there were the nights where death wasn't just a shadow; it was loud and close. I remember hearing gunshots while walking past an abandoned lot. The crack of bullets split the air, and instead of running I just stood there, listening as the chaos unfolded and faded into silence. My body didn't move, my heartbeat didn't spike. I just kept walking, as if nothing had happened. It was only when I got home that I realized how unnatural my reaction had been. I wasn't afraid. I wasn't even fazed.

The streets taught me that fear was a luxury I couldn't afford. If I let it in, it would paralyze me, control me even. But in losing fear, I also began to lose the natural human reactions that remind us of what's at stake. At times, I wondered if that numbness was strength or if it was hollowing me out. It kept me moving, kept me surviving, but was I losing pieces of myself in the process?

Through it all, I learned a profound lesson: numbness is a shield, but it can also be a cage. The streets taught me how to face danger without flinching and how to push through challenges without fear clouding my judgment. But they also showed me the cost of survival in a world where you can't afford to feel too much. The real strength wasn't just in the numbness itself but in learning how to harness it. I had to learn when to let the shield drop, when to feel, when to reconnect with the parts of myself I'd walled off. That's what East St. Louis taught me: to walk the fine line between survival and humanity, to protect myself without losing myself, to keep moving forward while holding onto hope that there was more waiting for me on the other side.

Chapter 2

THE BATTLES WITHIN: PERSONAL STRUGGLES
Wrestling with Identity, Self-Doubt, and External Pressures

T here was no moment of realization, no defining second when I understood we were poor. It was a quiet truth, hidden in the way my mother stretched meals and in the way we learned to be grateful for what little we had. But the world had its way of exposing truths, no matter how much love tried to shield them. I saw it in the way my friends got dropped off in freshly washed cars while I walked miles home, dodging the cracks in the sidewalks that mirrored the cracks forming inside me. I heard it in the excited chatter of classmates planning for homecoming, their biggest worry being what color their date's dress would be while I knew I couldn't even afford a ticket.

School field trips were out of the question. Sports teams came with fees that didn't exist in my world. The first time I saw kids trading lunch money like it was nothing, I felt something crack inside me. Money was a language I didn't speak, a currency that determined who belonged and who didn't. And I didn't. At home, my mother carried the weight of the world on her shoulders, and I hated seeing it. The way she sat at the table, staring at bills as if she could-will them away. The way she sometimes ate less so we could have more. That's when I started stealing. Not because I wanted to. Because I had to. Because the empty fridge didn't care about right or wrong. Because my mother's exhaustion didn't deserve more weight. The first time I stuffed food into my coat and walked out of a store, my heart pounded so loudly I swore the cashier could hear it. The guilt came later, but so did the relief, at least for that night, we wouldn't go hungry. This process was repeated hundreds of times by my siblings and I. We were not proud of what we were doing, it was just necessary to survive. Stores weren't the only victim; we would also steal from fruit trees in neighbors' yards. Yes, East St. Louis had fruit trees. My grandmother had fruit trees as well, but they all died off over time.

OVERCOMING NEGATIVE INFLUENCES AND PEER EXPECTATIONS

When the world shut doors in my face, I found my way into the places that didn't ask for money upfront such as the Lessie Bates Davis Neighborhood House and the Boys Club of East St. Louis. Along with other places where I met men like Wesley "Butch" Brown and Dennis Brooks, men who saw something in me that I struggled to see in myself. They allowed me to play little league football and AAU basketball for free, giving me a chance when so many others had only given me obstacles. But even there, battles followed me. My grandmother didn't want me to play sports. I'm not sure if it was out of weariness or stubbornness that she tripped off my heart murmur and about what might happen if I pushed too hard. I tried to explain that I needed it, that for a few hours on that field or on the court, I wasn't the kid who didn't have enough. I was just a kid, period. She didn't care to hear it. The result was that I now had to sneak around to play sports until I got caught and punished.

Then there were the fights. People thought I fought because I was angry. They thought I was reckless, dangerous, a problem to be contained. But they never asked why. I fought because I couldn't stand seeing someone get beaten down while the world watched. I fought because I knew what it felt like to be powerless, and I refused to let someone else feel that way. It didn't matter if I knew them or not. If I saw someone being bullied, I stepped in. But that came at a hefty price. Teachers stopped seeing the protector and started seeing the problem. My name became synonymous with trouble, and suddenly, I wasn't a kid with potential, I was just another black boy headed toward a dead end.

THE MOMENTS THAT NEARLY BROKE ME

There were moments; dark, suffocating moments when I thought about giving up. Moments when I wondered if I was meant to be another statistic, another name whispered in past tense.

The Detention Center —The first time I sat behind a locked door, I felt something inside me crack. The walls were cold, the silence suffocating. I wasn't there because I had stolen or hurt someone. I was there because I refused to stand by while a smaller kid got stomped out. But none of that mattered to the cops. All they saw was another black boy swinging, another one who added to their paperwork, so because it was recorded, they were angry and someone had to pay. Guess who that was?

Losing Friends to the Streets—The first time I saw a very close friend in a casket (Latrell "Peanut" Lucas - RIP), I couldn't breathe. The streets didn't have mercy. One by one, I lost people; some to bullets, some to drugs, and some to a system that was never designed to let them win. We didn't get grief counseling back then. I am not sure if it was even heard of, especially for a person who didn't have the resources. We just kept moving, kept swallowing the pain until it became part of us. I stopped counting the funerals and stopped letting myself feel too much. Because feeling meant hurting, and I didn't have time for that.

Being jailed and accused of a crime I didn't commit in Madison County—College was supposed to be my way out. My chance to rewrite the story. But when I was accused of residential burglary on the campus of SIU-Edwardsville, it felt like someone had reached into my chest and ripped the air from my lungs. I knew I was innocent, but innocence didn't mean much when the world or the law had already decided who you were.

Academic Probation in undergrad and SIU-Carbondale—School was my escape, but it was also a battlefield. I struggled to keep up, balancing the weight of my past with the expectations of my future and worrying about being sent back home as a failure. Then, in my doctoral program, the accusation came as plagiarism. After everything I had survived, after clawing my way up from a life that should have broken me, I was accused of stealing words. The irony burned. I had spent my whole life fighting to be heard, and now, someone was saying my voice wasn't my own.

One mistake, one misstep, and I would lose everything I had fought for. Being fired because of my past, no matter how hard I worked; my past followed me like a shadow. Jobs disappeared the moment background checks came back. Employers saw what I had done but never asked why or what happened. They saw the boy who had stolen, fought, and struggled, but not the man I had become.

THE WEIGHT OF IT ALL – *How Life Broke My Self-Esteem*

Growing up the way I did, moving through life with hardship as my shadow, I learned to survive before I learned to dream. But survival came at a cost, a deep, gnawing insecurity that settled in my bones long before I even knew what self-worth meant. For years, I walked through life feeling like I was already playing from behind, like I had been set up to lose before I even had a chance to start. And when you grow up feeling like life is against you, you start believing that maybe you are the problem.

A LIFE THAT TAUGHT ME I WASN'T ENOUGH

Being poor wasn't just about lacking money, it was about lacking value in the eyes of the world. Every time I had to say, "I can't afford it," it chipped away at me. I didn't just feel like I was missing out; I felt like I was less than the kids who had what I didn't. They were invited, included, and chosen. I was overlooked, left behind. I saw it in the way teachers treated the kids who came to school in new clothes while I showed up in the same pair of shoes for years, trying to mask the wear with shoe polish. I heard it in the way people whispered about me, labeling me before they even knew my name.

That boy fights too much. He won't make it far. Another troubled kid from East St. Louis. I told myself I didn't care, but that was a lie. I carried their words like weights, letting them define me even when I swore, they didn't. I learned to hide the pain, to wear toughness like a mask. But behind that mask was a boy who felt invisible. A boy who questioned his worth every single day.

FIGHTING BATTLES THAT WEREN'T ALWAYS PHYSICAL

I fought a lot, but the biggest battles were the ones no one saw. I fought the feeling of not belonging, like I was an outsider in every room I entered. When I was young, it was about not having the right clothes, not having money for school events and not fitting in with the kids who didn't have to think about survival. As I got older, it became more than that. I didn't feel smart enough. No matter how much I studied, no matter how many books I read, there was always a voice in my head whispering, you're not built for this. You're just lucky to be here. I didn't feel worthy enough. I worked harder than most just to prove that I belonged in spaces that weren't made for me, but it never felt like enough. No matter how much I accomplished, I still felt like the same boy who had once been handcuffed, the same kid who had stolen food to help keep his family from starving.

I didn't feel good enough for relationships. I struggled to trust, struggled to believe that I was worth being loved past my family. I thought people only saw my mistakes, my past, my struggle. I thought they saw the broken pieces of me and decided I wasn't worth the effort. And because I didn't believe in myself, I let people treat me however they wanted. I let jobs fire me without fighting back. I let people assume the worst about me without correcting them. I let rejection sink into my skin like I deserved it.

THE DARK PLACES IT TOOK ME

There were nights when I didn't want to wake up. Nights when the weight of everything; the losses, the failures, and the shame felt too heavy to carry. Nights when I questioned if I had already lost the battle before I even had a chance to win.

I couldn't see a future for myself. I had spent so long surviving that I didn't know how to live. I had spent so long fighting to prove my worth that I wasn't even sure I had any.

THE HARDENING OF A SOMEWHAT SHY, DELICATE, STRUGGLING BOY

Growing up in East St. Louis wasn't a childhood it was a battlefield. Every single day felt like a fight for survival, and if you didn't adapt, the streets would devour you whole. There were no safe spaces, no moments of reprieve. You either became the predator, or you stayed the prey. I learned that lesson young, and though it wasn't a path I chose, it shaped me into someone I never thought I'd become.

It all began in the fourth grade, the year I came face-to-face with fear for the first time. The sixth-grade bullies had marked me, and there was no escape. They were relentless, cornering me every day and demanding lunch money (35 cents) I didn't have. Thirty-five cents was a lot during that time. My family was poor, and by society's standards, dirt poor. Every cent mom made was used to keep the lights on or put food on the table. But bullies don't care about that. They don't care about anything but their power. They smelled the weakness on me, and they thrived on it.

School was coming to an end and I was nearing my freedom, the day I finally escaped their grip. I tried to slip out of the building unnoticed, keeping my head down and my steps quiet. But they were waiting for me. Their fists came down like thunder, pounding me until I couldn't feel where the pain ended, and my body began. I couldn't fight back, I didn't know how. They dragged my limp, bruised body to an old, abandoned basement, the kind of place you only see in nightmares. The smell of mildew and rot choked me as they left me there, laughing, as if my life didn't matter. And for a moment, I believed them. I thought I was going to die there.

But something inside me refused to quit. I clawed my way out, inch by inch, dragging my broken body into the daylight. By the time I made it home, I looked like I'd been through a war. My mom's face fell when she saw me. "What happened to you?" she demanded, her voice trembling. I lied. "I fell off the monkey bars," I said. It took every ounce of strength in me to hold back the tears of hurt and anger. Although she didn't press me, my second-oldest brother wasn't so easily fooled. My second oldest brother was a vicious person. I don't even remember or know how he had gotten that way. I think I missed some things growing up in the same house as him. He cornered me, his eyes sharp and unrelenting. "Tell me the truth punk," he said. And I did. Let's just say, I unleashed the "Kraken." That next school day, LAWD-HAM-MERCY," my brother brought HELL with him. What he unleashed put fear in every spectator watching. Those bullies learned the meaning of karma and I never saw them again at school.

But something inside me had changed. That beating had stripped me of my innocence and replaced it with a simmering rage, a determination never to be powerless again. It hardened a once shy, yet delicate boy to the struggle. I spent that summer hardening myself, not just physically but mentally. I thought about every moment I had been humiliated, every time I had felt small or weak. And I vowed never again to let anyone make me feel that way.

When fifth grade started, I wasn't the same person. I walked into that classroom with my head held high and my shoulders squared. The kids who had once laughed at me, who had chased me home on the last day of school, who disrespected me as a patrol boy, saw something different in my eyes. They didn't know what had changed, but they knew better than to test me. I had become a fighter not just for myself, but for anyone who needed someone to stand up for them. And Mrs. Eckford (who over saw the Student Patrol Program) realized this change almost instantly, so she named me Captain of the school Patrol. No one crossed me, plus-- I had mixed in with some tuff guys in other classes. So, let's just say that my influence had grown with people of like mind.

But with that transformation came something darker. I had become what I feared most: a bully. Not the kind who preyed on the weak, but the kind who hunted the hunters. If I saw someone being picked on, I stepped in, and I made sure the bully knew what it felt like to be on the other side. I became a protector, a physical spokesperson for the voiceless. But there was a part of me that reveled in the power, in the respect I commanded. I had tasted what it felt like to be feared, and I loved it.

By no stretch of the imagination am I saying that I was the toughest person in East St. Louis, I wasn't trying to be. Besides, I was definitely no match for my third oldest brother. But I was well respected, and there weren't too many people willing to test me. Those who did learned quickly that I wasn't the same kid who had been dragged into that basement and gotten the beat down of his life. I wasn't the same boy who had tied a girl's hair to a table leg out of spite or who had been chased home by his entire class. I had changed. The streets had shaped me, turned me into someone who could stand tall in a world that wanted to crush me.

But with all that respect and power came the realization that I had walked a dangerous line. I had let my pain, my anger, and my fear mold me into a terror of my own. I justified it because I wasn't targeting the weak, I was defending them. But deep down, I knew I was feeding the same beast that had once preyed on me. That realization was the beginning of my reform. I didn't want to be remembered as a bully, even one with a righteous cause. I wanted to be something better, someone stronger, not just in my fists, but in my heart.

East St. Louis taught me hard lessons. It taught me that respect wasn't given, it was earned. It taught me that power, unchecked, can corrupt even the best intentions. And it taught me that survival isn't just about fighting, it's about knowing when to let go of the fight and build something better. By the time I left elementary school, I wasn't just a fighter or a survivor. I was someone who had been broken and rebuilt, someone who had faced the worst and come out on the other side. The streets didn't defeat me, they forged me. And I made sure that, in the end, I used what the streets gave me to become more than just a product of my environment. I became something greater.

There was no space for softness in me. Every time I thought about trusting someone, I remembered how easy it was to get stabbed in the back. Every time I thought about asking for help, I remembered how people looked at me when I came to school smelling like kerosene, my stomach growling loud enough for the whole class to hear. That's when I stopped letting people get close. I built walls. Thick ones. By the time I hit high school at East St. Louis Senior High, I was already seasoned. I had been locked up at the Cherry Hill Juvenile Detention Center quite a bit for fighting, stealing, skipping school. I smoked weed like it was nothing, because when reality is too sharp, you do whatever you can to dull the edges. But deep down, I knew I was standing on a ledge. One wrong step, and I was going to fall straight into the same pit that had swallowed so many boys before me. The streets ain't love nobody. The streets will chew you up and spit you out. And I was starting to wonder, was that all there was for me? Was I just another statistic, another body waiting to be buried? Or was there something else? Something more? I didn't know the answer yet. But I knew one thing, if I wanted to live, I had to find a way out.

CLIMBING OUT OF THE DARKNESS

Self-worth didn't come easy when life had spent years convincing you that you don't have any. It took years of unlearning, of rewiring my thoughts, of forcing myself to believe that I was more than my past. It took people seeing something in me when I couldn't see it in myself. It took standing in front of a mirror and saying, you are enough, even when I didn't believe it. I had to fight for my self-esteem the way I had fought for everything else in my life. I had to rebuild myself, piece by piece, learning to love the parts of me that the world had once told me were unworthy.

I am still learning. But now, I know one thing for sure, I was never less than. I was always more. Although the world didn't want me to see it, I persevered. There were nights when I lay awake, staring at the ceiling, wondering if I was supposed to fail. Wondering if life was always going to be this hard. But something inside me refused to break. I had seen too much, lost too much, to give in. I had fought too hard to turn back. The world had tried to tell me who I was. But I was more than a kid who stole to survive. More than a boy who fought because he couldn't stand injustice.

More than a troubled youth who people expected to end up in the system. I was more. And I was going to prove it.

Chapter 3

TURNING POINTS AND TOUGH CHOICES

The Crossroads: *A Different Path vs The Same Path*

The weight of expectation wasn't just heavy, it was crushing, like a 500-pound weight pressing against my chest, daring me to breathe. Every morning in East St. Louis, I woke up with the same reality staring me in the face: society had already decided my fate. A black boy. Born into struggle. Destined for the streets, a jail cell, or worse. It was a script already written for me, and every day felt like a battle to keep from playing the role they expected me to fill. The streets had a way of making you feel like you belonged. They promised fast money, respect, and survival, three things that seemed more tangible than a future I couldn't yet see. I watched my older cousins, their pockets fat with cash, living the kind of life that seemed glamorous until it wasn't. Some got locked up. Others disappeared, their names whispered like ghost stories of what could happen if you stayed too long, and/or played the game too hard. As I got older, I had teachers whispering something else, something different. You're smart. You've got potential. You can be more. It sounded good, but the streets didn't reward patience. A diploma couldn't put food on the table overnight. Success through education felt like a long, uncertain road with no guarantee at the end.

I found sports. At first, it was just a way to burn off energy, an excuse to stay out of trouble a little longer. But the more I played, the more I felt something shift inside me. Sports gave me something the streets never could, discipline, structure, and a reason to push myself beyond what I thought was possible. For the first time, I started to feel something I hadn't felt in a long time: pride. My grandmother wasn't having it, though. She forbade me from playing, convinced that I needed to focus on school and church. But I found ways around it. I snuck in practices, and played in games when she thought I was somewhere else. And when I stepped onto that field or court, I wasn't just another black boy trying to outrun his fate, I was somebody. Coaches like Butch and Dennis saw it too. They saw the fire in me, the hunger. They saw a kid standing at the edge, one bad decision away from losing himself. They pulled me aside after practice and spoke to me like I mattered. They told me I could go further than the streets, further than East St. Louis, if I just stayed focused. And for the first time, I started to believe them.

THE PEOPLE WHO BELIEVED IN ME WHEN I COULDN'T SEE MY OWN WORTH

It's one thing to have teachers telling me that I was special. But when the custodians, the cafeteria workers, the people who saw me when nobody else was looking, pulled me aside, that's when I knew it was real. Ms. Jay, the custodian who worked late into the night, used to stop me when I was wandering the halls after school. "Boy, you walking like you lost," she'd say, shaking her head. "Ain't nothing for you out there but trouble. You got too much in you to waste it." Mr. Taylor, who worked on the cafeteria serving line, would slide extra food onto my tray, giving me a look that said he knew my stomach wasn't the only thing empty, I was starving for something bigger, something I couldn't quite name yet.

THE CHOSEN ONE

Going to church? That wasn't optional. It was law. You went, no questions asked. And to make things even more interesting, my uncle was the pastor, so there was no ducking out early and no skipping. For some strange reason, my family started looking at me differently, treating me like; The One. The one who was going to make it. The one who would climb heights no one else had reached. The one who was going to break the cycle. At first, I laughed it off. But the more they said it, the more serious it became. It wasn't just words anymore, it was expectation. My brothers and sisters started looking at me differently. It wasn't just admiration; it was pressure. They were watching, waiting, counting on me. My mother, my grandmother, my father, uncles, aunts, cousins and even neighborhood alligators (the guys who ruled the neighborhoods) didn't let me slide. When I messed up, they didn't just punish me; they made sure I understood. "You ain't like the rest of them," my grandmother would say. "GOD put something different in you. Don't you waste it."

I remember the day my father found out I skipped class to hang out. He didn't yell. He didn't even get mad. He just looked at me, and the disappointment in his eyes was worse than any punishment he could've given me. "You think this is a game? You think you got time to play?" His voice was low, controlled. "You don't get to be like them. You understand me? You got something they don't got. Don't you waste it." I wanted to be mad. I wanted to push back. But deep down, I knew he was right. I couldn't waste it.

A BLESSING AROUND THE CORNER THAT CHANGED MY VIEW OF THINGS

As a teenager, I spent a lot of time at the Central City Homes, working alongside my boy. We weren't getting paid, but we stayed busy picking up trash, shoveling snow, helping fix up apartments, anything that kept us moving, out of trouble and out of the streets. To the apartment manager, Ms. Carol Paige, I must have looked like the most well-mannered, hardworking young man she'd ever met. But what she didn't know was that I wasn't doing it just to be nice. My mother's health was failing, and our living conditions were beyond rough. I was just trying to keep myself occupied, stay out of trouble, stay out of the house, and maybe, just maybe, find a way to help my family. Then one day, Ms. Paige called me into her office. "Who are your parents?" she asked. "Where do you live?" I hesitated. Not because I was scared but because I knew the truth was ugly. Our home wasn't the kind of place you wanted people to know about. The last thing I needed was a pity party. So, I dodged the question, shrugged it off, and kept it moving. But life has a funny way of forcing you to face the things you try to hide.

THE SURPRISE VISIT

That Monday after school, I walked into our house, expecting the usual; dim lights, the smell of struggle lingering in the air, the weight of barely making it press down on my mother's-tired shoulders. But what I didn't expect was to see Ms. Paige sitting in our living room, deep in conversation with my mom. My stomach dropped. Damn. What the hell is going on here? They talked for what felt like forever, and I sat there, trying to make myself invisible. I knew I hadn't done anything wrong, but growing up the way I did, you learned really quick that unexpected visits could mean bad news. When Ms. Paige finally got up to leave, my mother gave me the look. The kind that could freeze time and send shivers down your spine. The kind that said, boy, what the hell have you been out here telling people about our business? I didn't know what Ms. Paige had said to her, but whatever it was, it had stirred something deep.

A HOME OF OUR OWN

A little while after that, Ms. Paige pulled up outside and told me and my mother to get in the car. No explanation. Just, "Come on, I want to show y'all something." We drove through the Central City Homes until we pulled up to 1380 Walter. It was an empty, well-kept, large, beautiful apartment. A real apartment. Ms. Paige turned to my mother and asked, "What do you think?" My mom, still unsure of what was happening, glanced around and said, "It's nice." Then Ms. Paige handed her a set of keys. My mom frowned. "What are these for?" Ms. Paige smiled. "They're yours. This is your apartment." My mother shook her head, already preparing to refuse. "I can't afford this." And then Ms. Paige said something that changed everything. "I sit in my office every day and watch your son shovel snow, pick up trash, help our maintenance men clean apartments, and never once ask for a dime. He's probably paid your rent a hundred times over. The least we can do is offer you this apartment, rent-free." I didn't even know how to react. I was just standing there, trying to process what had just happened. Then my mother turned to me, her eyes filled with something I hadn't seen in a long time, relief. She hugged me so tightly I thought she was never going to let go. It hit me. I had done the unthinkable, yet unintentional. I had gotten my family out of the basement, out of the infestation, out of the darkness. I had given them something better. More importantly, I had made my mom proud, something I can never remember doing and it FELT ABSOLUTELY AMAZING!!!

MORE THAN JUST A BLESSING

But the blessings didn't stop there. A few weeks later, we found out something crazy, Ms. Paige wasn't just some random apartment manager. She was family. She and my mother were cousins. And to top it off, she later became my Godmother. And trust me, she was no joke. She wasn't just going to let us slip into bad habits or take this blessing for granted. She held us accountable, helped my mother keep us in line, made sure we understood the value of what we had been given. For the first time in a long time, my world was getting better. For the first time, I started to believe that maybe, just maybe I really could make it out. Carol and my mom remained extremely close until mom went to paradise.

MAKING THE CHOICE TO PURSUE A DIFFERENT PATH

The night I made my decision wasn't some dramatic Hollywood moment. It was me, standing in my mother's living room, looking at her tired face, knowing that I had the power to either add to her burdens or take them away. I was tired of barely making it. Tired of surviving instead of living. It was me, walking through my old neighborhood and realizing that I was standing at the same crossroads that had swallowed so many before me. It was me, understanding that if I stayed, I would never leave again. I prayed for yet another chance. I had never prayed my way out of a situation before and this was my first. I knew that if given another chance that I couldn't be the same person I had been before. If I wanted another shot, I had to be better. I had to shed the mindset that had nearly destroyed me. So, I humbled myself, understanding that basketball wasn't my only way out, education was. This time, I wasn't just surviving, I was fighting to win. I thought about something my Aunt Jeanette had told me. She was the kind of woman who didn't take nonsense, the one person who always seemed to understand what I was up against. One day, she mentioned Lane College, an HBCU. A place where kids like me, kids who weren't supposed to make it went to prove everyone wrong. I thought about my boys, the ones still in the game, still chasing ghosts. Some of them wouldn't live to see 25. Some of them already had rap sheets too thick to escape. I wasn't better than them. I wasn't special. But I had been given a different kind of chance. I didn't sleep that night. My mind raced, replaying every moment, every warning, every whispered promise of the streets telling me I'd never make it out. But when the sun rose, I made a decision. I wasn't going to be a statistic. I wasn't going to be another name on a forgotten list. I was going to take the long road, the one filled with uncertainty, struggle, and obstacles. The one where I had to work twice as hard and prove myself repeatedly. The next time I saw Aunt Jeanette, I told her, "I have to make this happen." That was the moment I chose to rewrite my story. And I never looked back.

Chapter 4
EDUCATION AS A WEAPON
Enrolling at Lane College: *The HBCU That Changed My Life*

If the streets were a battlefield, then education was my sword, my armor, and my only real chance of survival. I didn't know it yet, not when I first stepped onto the campus of Lane College, an HBCU that would mold me, sharpen me, and set my soul on fire. I still remember that first day. The heat from the Tennessee sun pressed against my skin as I walked through the campus, my feet stepping onto history, onto the same paths where generations before me had fought for their right to an education. I could hear it in the whispers of the wind, in the walls of the buildings, in the voices of the professors who carried the weight of black excellence in their chests. Lane wasn't just a school. It was a sanctuary, a battleground where young Black men and women came to arm themselves with knowledge and take back the power that the world tried so hard to strip from us. But college wasn't just a dream realized; it was a war of its own. Coming from East St. Louis, I had already mastered the art of survival. I knew how to hustle, how to read people, how to move with purpose. But none of that prepared me for the grind of higher education. It wasn't the streets I was fighting anymore; it was myself. The doubts. The weight of expectations. The nights I lay awake staring at the ceiling, wondering if I really had what it took. My Lane College family didn't just expect me to just pass rigorous courses, they expected me to excel. They demanded I show up, be present, and engage. They saw something in me that I wasn't yet ready to claim.

I refused to go back home a failure. Some days, the struggle hit me harder than others. There were weeks when money was nonexistent, when the idea of eating anything other than ramen noodles or a few slices of bread felt like a fantasy.

There were moments when I stared at my books, exhausted, questioning whether it was all worth it. And then there was the pressure not just from school, but from home. My family was counting on me. My community was watching me. My people needed me to win. But I wasn't alone. I had brothers beside me, other young men from East St. Louis who had the same fire in their bellies, the same weight on their backs. J-Rock (RIH), Bobby Lewis (RIH), Harv (RIH), Chip Conners (RIH), Cal-Ross, Lil Butch, Flav (My Room-Dawg), Torrence, Shotgun, Fithy (Astro), Sneaky, Fly-Guy, City Spud, D-Nice, Floyd, Ronnie-Mo, Teeba, Boog, Chip Manley, and many other homeboys. We held each other up. Late-night study sessions turned into therapy sessions. We celebrated each other's wins, and when one of us fell, we picked him back up. We joned, acted silly, and most of all, we protected each other.

And then there was my fraternity, a sacred brotherhood that pushed me beyond my limits, that held me accountable, that made me sharper, stronger and wiser. The lessons I learned through them weren't just about scholarship and service, they were about bonding and perseverance, about making it in a world that didn't always want to see us succeed.

The men of Omega Psi Phi Fraternity Incorporated, Kappa Sigma Chapter were my brothers, especially that Spring 92' line, the Five Hounds From Hell (Delmos Cauley, Stanley Stubbs, Allen Lane, Eric Roberson and yours truly, Michael

Triplett). Lane College wasn't just where I earned a degree it was where I became a young man with promise.

FINDING MY VOICE, MY MENTORS, AND MY PURPOSE

Somewhere along the way, I stopped just going to college. I started becoming something greater. It was because of the people who poured into me, who refused to let me sit in the background and watch life pass me by. President Chambers, with his quiet yet commanding presence, made sure we understood that we were walking on sacred ground, that we were standing on the shoulders of our ancestors. Mr. and Mrs. Kirkendoll saw past the tough exterior, past the survival instincts, past the struggle. They reminded me that I wasn't invisible, that I mattered. Ms. Lovelady had a way of speaking life into me, even on the days when I was too stubborn to hear it. Dean Thomas made sure we knew that education wasn't just about passing classes, it was about power. It was about freedom.

I remember one conversation with Dean Thomas that shook me. He pulled me aside after reading one of my papers. "You know you're not just another student, right?", he asked. "You got a voice. A real one. You ever thought about using it?" I didn't know what to say. But for the first time, I felt like somebody. Dr. Jarmon, Mr. Thacker, Dean David, Dr. Garcia, Dr. Debnath, each played a role in shaping me, in pulling out the best parts of me. They weren't just professors. They were warriors in the fight for knowledge, pushing me into the light when the shadows of my past tried to pull me back. I found my voice in their classrooms. I found my purpose in their lessons. Lane College wasn't just an HBCU, it wasn't just a place of learning. It was a place of belonging. "Esse non Videri—to be, not to seem". It's where I realized that I wasn't just here for myself. I was here to lead, to uplift, and to inspire.

LEARNING LEADERSHIP THROUGH EDUCATION

Education wasn't just about getting a diploma, it was my weapon. It was my way out. But more importantly, it was my way back in, back into my community, back into my family, and back into the lives of the younger students coming behind me who needed someone to show them that making it wasn't just possible, it was expected. I became a mentor without even realizing it. Younger classmates started coming to me for guidance, for help with schoolwork, for advice on how to navigate the struggles of being a Black student in a world that still wasn't built for us. I started tutoring, not just because I was good at it, but because I had to. Because if I had fought this hard to make it, then it was my duty to reach back and make sure someone else did too. I took people under my wing, just like my mentors had done for me. I became the person I wished I had in my earlier years, the person who didn't just tell them to succeed, but showed them how.

AND WHEN DID I GO BACK HOME?

Oh, those trips back to East St. Louis were different. I wasn't just some kid trying to make it anymore, I was a storyteller, a witness, a promise. When I came back, the streets listened. My old friends, the ones still caught in the cycle, would pull up, dapping me up, telling me to "stay outta trouble" even though I had spent my whole life trying to do just that. They didn't let me slip. They protected me because I was their proof, their walking, breathing evidence that there was another way. I sent money home to my mom whenever I could, knowing that my success wasn't just mine, it was hers, too. Every sacrifice she made, every struggle she endured, every time she held us together when everything was falling apart, I paid her back the only way I knew how. I was making my mom, my family, and East St. Louis proud. And it felt amazing.

When I walked across that stage in May of 1993, I didn't just earn a degree. I earned freedom. I earned a future. I earned the right to stand in front of every young black boy coming up behind me and say: You don't have to be a statistic. You don't have to be what they expect you to be. You are more. And if I made it, so can you. Lane College didn't just change my life. It saved it.

Chapter 5

HARD ROAD TO LEADERSHIP

The road to educational leadership was long, winding, and often brutal. It's not for the faint of heart. It tests your patience, resilience, intelligence, and ability to withstand rejection, failure, and setbacks. For me, this journey wasn't just about earning degrees or collecting titles. It was about survival, proving something to myself, and never letting the circumstances I was born into become situations that defined where I would end up. But my journey wasn't just about me. In 1996, my life changed forever. I became a father for the second time. This time I had a daughter, and I was a single father at that. Suddenly, the fight wasn't just for my own success but for my daughter's future, too.

THE STRUGGLE OF BALANCING PERSONAL RESPONSIBILITIES AND CAREER ASPIRATIONS

After graduating from Lane College with my Bachelor of Science in Business Administration, I had high hopes, but like so many others, I quickly realized that having a degree didn't guarantee success. The world didn't roll out a red carpet for me. It handed me bills, responsibilities, and a demand for experience that I didn't have. Now add a baby girl to that equation. A tiny life completely dependent on me. I was at a crossroads, unsure of what I truly wanted to do. I knew I wanted to make an impact, but I also needed to make money fast. I bounced from job to job, desperately trying to find my niche. I wanted to be a teacher, but the pay was so bad it felt impossible to sustain myself and my daughter. On top of that, I couldn't pass the Praxis exam, the gateway to certification. I studied, retook the test, and failed again. That test became my nemesis. It felt like every time I took a step forward, life knocked me three steps back.

Bills didn't stop. Diapers, formula, doctor visits, being a parent didn't care that I was struggling to find my path. There were nights when I stared at my daughter while she slept, wondering how I was going to make it work. Then life took an even darker turn.

ROCK BOTTOM: *Homeless, Again Jailed, and Again Broken*

No one imagines their lowest moment. It just happens. One day, you're barely staying afloat, and the next, the ground beneath you collapses. I was already juggling fatherhood, multiple jobs, and trying to build a career, but the weight of a past child support case came crashing down on me. I was arrested. Jailed. Stripped of everything I had fought to hold onto. The world didn't care that I was actively raising my daughter. The system didn't care that I was a present father doing everything I could to provide for her. I was just another case number. Another statistic. And as if that wasn't enough, I lost everything, my home, my car, my sense of stability. I went bankrupt.

For the first time in my life, I was truly homeless. I had nothing but the clothes on my back. My furniture was in one of my friend's basements and I was determined not to let this moment define me. I could have folded. Many would have. But

I refused. And when I had nothing left, God showed me I wasn't alone.

One of my best friends to this day stepped in and gave my daughter and I a place to stay. He didn't judge me. He didn't make me feel less than a man. He opened his home, reminding me that even in my darkest hour, I wasn't alone. He would not accept a red cent from me.

THE WEIGHT OF LOSS ON THE ROAD TO LEADERSHIP

Loss is an inevitability of life, yet nothing could have prepared me for the profound impact of losing my mother, my fuel source, my anchor, the very embodiment of my drive. She was not just a guiding force; she was the unwavering light that illuminated my path, pushing me forward in moments of doubt, exhaustion, and uncertainty.

Her absence is more than grief, it is a void, a deafening silence in the moments where her wisdom, reassurance, and strength once stood. Leadership, at its core, demands resilience, vision, and unyielding determination, but when the foundation that fortified those very qualities is suddenly gone, the burden of the journey becomes exponentially heavier.

This loss was not just emotional; it became a psychological weight pressing down on my ability to lead with clarity and conviction. Every decision, every challenge, every obstacle now came with an added layer of solitude, a reminder that the person who once helped me navigate storms was no longer there. It would have been easy to let grief become a roadblock, to allow the pain to deter me from the path I had been walking.

But leadership is not about avoiding hardship, it is about enduring it, learning from it, and finding a way to transform pain into purpose. Though my mother's physical presence was/is gone, her influence remains woven into the fabric of

79

who I am. She did not raise me to crumble under adversity. She prepared me for it, even when I did not realize it at the time.

Yes, the road to leadership became lonelier, heavier, and infinitely more challenging after her passing. The weight of loss threatened to derail me completely. But with honoring her memory, I found my second wind. I realized that the greatest tribute I could give her was not succumbing to the setback but using it as fuel to propel me forward, just as she always had.

Her absence reshaped my leadership, making it more intentional, more reflective, and ultimately, more resilient. It taught me that true strength is not found in the absence of pain, but in the ability to carry it and keep moving forward.

That time in my life was humbling beyond words. I went from being the man others depended on to feeling like I had failed at everything, fatherhood, my career, and my dreams. But the fire inside me never went out. Instead, I fought harder.

THE CLIMB BACK UP: *From The Bottom To The Top*

With nothing but faith and determination, I rebuilt. I took whatever jobs I could, working tirelessly to get back on my feet. I poured every ounce of pain into my studies, determined to finish what I had started. It wasn't just about advanced degrees that I had received, it was about proving to myself that I was more than my setbacks. That the world did not get to decide my fate, I did.

I clawed my way back, from substitute teaching to school social worker, assistant principal, principal, turnaround specialist, and eventually, superintendent. Every step up the ladder, I carried those experiences with me, the humiliation of hitting rock bottom, the hunger of struggling to provide, and the pain of being counted out. Instead of letting them break me, I let them fuel me.

LESSONS IN HUMILITY, PERSEVERANCE, AND DISCIPLINE

East St. Louis made me. It hardened me, but it also humbled me. Growing up, I saw struggle firsthand, and I understood that failure wasn't the end of the road, it was just part of the journey. I failed more times than I can count. I failed exams. I failed interviews. I failed at things that others seemed to breeze through effortlessly. But every time I failed, I got back up.

Perseverance became my greatest weapon. Discipline kept me focused. When the doubt crept in, when the rejection stung, when the pressure felt unbearable. I kept going. I didn't have the luxury of giving up. I learned the power of humility, how to accept help when I needed it and how to lift others as I climbed. I learned the power of perseverance

--that no matter how bad things get, as long as you keep moving, you're never truly defeated. I learned that discipline wasn't just about work, it was about survival. It was about getting up when every part of you wanted to stay down.

THE MESSAGE: *My Story Is Proof That You Can Rise*

My journey to educational leadership wasn't glamorous. It was ugly. It was painful. It was filled with losses that most people don't recover from. But every hardship, every long night of studying, every moment of doubt led me here. I fought for my seat at the table, and I earned it. Now, as I look back, I realize my struggle wasn't just for me. It was for my daughter, so she could see firsthand what resilience looks like. It was for my students so they would know they could break the cycle of struggle. It was for every single person who has ever felt like the world counted them out. This road was never meant to be easy. But if I could rise from the lowest point in my life and make it to the top, so can you.

Chapter 6

BECOMING THE CHANGE

L eadership is more than a title or a position, it is a responsibility, a call to action, and in many ways, a burden. When I stepped into my first major leadership role, I quickly realized that the weight of responsibility was heavier than I had imagined. It was no longer just about me, my success, my growth, or my aspirations. Now, I was accountable for others: their development, their challenges, and their potential. I saw myself in the students I served, and that realization changed everything.

SEEING MYSELF IN THE STUDENTS: *Breaking Cycles Of Struggle*

Walking the hallways, stepping into classrooms, and engaging with students, I saw reflections of my past. Faces filled with untapped potential but, weighed down by circumstances beyond their control. Some carried the scars of poverty, others the burden of fractured families, and many the silent struggles of being underestimated. I knew their stories because, in many ways, they mirrored my own.

Instead of simply offering sympathy, I used my personal experiences to build relatability. I knew what it felt like to be overlooked, to battle self-doubt, and to push against a system that seemed indifferent. But I also knew the power of persistence, the strength found in community, and the importance of having someone who truly sees you. That became my mission, to see them, to validate their experiences, and to show them that their past did not have to define their future.

Breaking cycles of struggle meant more than providing encouragement; it meant creating tangible opportunities for growth. It required challenging old narratives, dismantling limiting beliefs, and equipping students with tools to rewrite their own stories. I made it my business to be present, to listen, and to remind them that they were capable of more than the world had told them they were.

CHALLENGING THE SYSTEM: *Advocating For The Overlooked*

Leadership, for me, has never been about maintaining the status quo. Systems, by nature, are built to function efficiently, but efficiency often comes at the cost of individuality. Too many students, especially those labeled as "difficult" or "incorrigible," fall through the cracks, and like me, written off before they ever have a chance to prove otherwise. I refused to let that happen on my watch.

I have always been a protector. Since childhood, I found myself standing up for those who couldn't stand up for themselves. That instinct never faded, it only evolved. As a leader, I saw my role as more than just guiding policies or managing operations; I saw it as advocacy. I fought for the forgotten children, the students who had been pushed aside, and the ones whose potential had been ignored in favor of discipline referrals and exclusionary tactics.

Advocating for them meant challenging outdated disciplinary models, pushing for restorative justice practices, and demanding that educators see students as whole individuals, not just test scores or behavioral problems. It meant standing in board meetings, confronting decision-makers, and sometimes making myself unpopular in the process. But leadership isn't about popularity, it's about purpose. And my purpose was clear: to fight for those who couldn't fight for themselves.

THE POWER OF MENTORSHIP: *Lifting Others As I Climbed*

True leadership isn't about climbing alone. It's about bringing others up with you. Throughout my journey, I have been fortunate to have mentors who saw potential in me when I couldn't see it in myself. They guided me, corrected me, and inspired me to reach higher. I owed it to them, and to myself, to pay that forward.

Mentorship became one of the most rewarding aspects of my leadership. I invested in both students and staff, sharing my journey with transparency and honesty. I didn't just offer advice; I shared my failures, my missteps, and the lessons I learned along the way. Because leadership isn't about projecting perfection, it's about modeling resilience.

For students, mentorship means showing them that someone believed in them, that they were more than their circumstances, and that success was possible with discipline and determination. For staff, it means fostering a culture of growth, encouraging them to challenge themselves, and creating an environment where they felt seen and valued.

Lifting others as I climb isn't just a philosophy, it is a practice. I made it a priority to create pathways for those coming behind me, helping others make themselves more marketable by ensuring that they had opportunities to grow, lead, and eventually surpass me. Because the true measure of leadership isn't how far I go, it's how many people I bring with me.

BECOMING THE CHANGE

I didn't step into leadership expecting it to be easy. I knew the weight of responsibility would be heavy, but I also knew that change was necessary. Becoming the change meant refusing to accept mediocrity, challenging systems that no longer served their purpose, and standing in the gap for those who had been left behind.

It meant seeing myself in the students I served, using my own story as a tool for connection and transformation. It meant being a protector, an advocate, and a relentless force for those often ignored. And above all, it meant ensuring that leadership was never just about me, it was about creating a legacy of empowerment, resilience, and unwavering commitment to those who needed it most.

The journey was never meant to be easy, but then again, nothing worth fighting for ever is.

Chapter 7
FROM THE STREETS OF EAST ST. LOUIS TO OFFICE OF THE SUPERINTENDENT

The road from the streets of East St. Louis to the Office of the Superintendent wasn't paved in privilege or ease. It was a battleground, one where struggle was an everyday reality, where failure threatened to swallow ambition whole, and where obstacles were placed not as mere challenges, but as full-fledged barriers meant to stop progress. But if my journey has taught me anything, it's that survival is a skill, and resilience is a weapon. I have fought my way through, scraping and clawing past the circumstances that sought to define me, and through every trial, I emerged stronger, more determined, and unwilling to accept anything less than victory.

THE HARD ROAD OUT OF EAST ST. LOUIS

East St. Louis is a place that shapes you. It teaches you lessons most people don't learn until adulthood, how to navigate danger, how to read people, and how to survive when the odds are stacked against you. It's a city with a history of struggle and successes, a place where opportunity doesn't come knocking; you must break down doors to find it.

Growing up here meant knowing loss early, understanding that dreams could be stolen if you weren't careful. It meant watching friends take the wrong paths and knowing that one wrong decision could change your entire future. It meant seeing promise fade into disappointment because the system was never built to save us, it was built to contain us.

BUT I REFUSED TO BE CONTAINED

Even when the world told me that my circumstances would define my ceiling, I believed otherwise. I wasn't naïve to the struggles around me, but I refused to accept that they would be my story's ending. Football became my escape, my discipline, my proving ground. It gave me purpose when the streets threatened to pull me in. On that field, I learned about teamwork, about sacrifice, and about how to take a hit and still get back up. It was more than a sport it was survival training for life.

COLLEGE: THE FIGHT CONTINUES

Leaving East St. Louis for college didn't mean leaving the struggle behind. The challenges didn't disappear, they just evolved. College wasn't easy. I wasn't just competing academically; I was battling self-doubt, financial instability, and the weight of expectations. There were days I questioned whether I belonged, whether the system was meant for someone like me. I made mistakes. I failed. And there were times when it felt like the walls were closing in, ready to send me right back to where I came from.

THE LONG ROAD TO SUPERINTENDENCY:
A Battle of Integrity, Resilience, and Purpose

A WAR OF PERSISTENCE

Stepping into leadership didn't happen overnight. I wasn't handed the keys to the district with applause or open arms. No, leadership was a battle, one where persistence was my weapon, and resilience was my armor. I wasn't just fighting to climb the ranks. I was fighting against perceptions, biases, and systemic resistance. I was fighting against those who looked at where I came from and assumed I wasn't fit to sit at the table. Every rejection, every time I was overlooked, every time my ideas were dismissed, I fought back not with words, but with results.

I proved myself repeatedly. Not because I had to, but because I refused to let others define my worth. I fought for students the way I once fought for myself. I challenged policies that failed them, systems that overlooked them, and leadership that was too comfortable maintaining the status quo. I mentored young men and women who needed someone to tell them they mattered, that they had a future, that their circumstances were not their destiny. I stood in the gap for those who had no advocate. And for that, I was met with opposition. But I refused to play politics. I refused to be complacent. I refused to let the system dictate who could and could not succeed.

THAT DAMN JOURNEY

My journey from the streets of East St. Louis to the superintendent's office wasn't just about career advancement, it was a test of will, character and unshakable determination. I didn't just make it here; I fought my way here. Growing up in a community where opportunity was scarce, but strength was abundant, I learned early that survival wasn't just about endurance, it was about strategy, adaptability, and knowing when to stand firm. Those same lessons guided me through every stage of my professional ascent from substitute teacher to social worker, from assistant principal to principal, and finally, to district leader and superintendent. Each position shaped me, tested me, and strengthened me. Every challenge forced me to sharpen my leadership, my vision, and my resolve.

But with success came something else: Resistance. The Target on My Back, Defamation and Scrutiny

As I climbed, the attacks followed. Colleagues, community members, and even decision-makers, many of whom should have been allies became obstacles. Some of them weren't just skeptical of change; they feared it. They feared the shifts I brought, the accountability I demanded, and the progress I represented. Rather than acknowledge the turnaround efforts, the improved student achievement, and the structural reforms, they resorted to character assassination. False narratives, whispered doubts, deliberate distortions of my record, all aimed at discrediting the work. They ignored the facts: Millions saved through financial audits that exposed wasteful spending. Student literacy rates rising, with over 70% of kindergartners reading at or above grade level. Discipline reforms cutting suspensions and expulsions, creating safer, more supportive learning environments. Assessment protocols ensuring that over 90% of students received data-driven instruction. Increased graduation rates, reduced dropout rates, and a district on the rise. But instead of acknowledging this progress, they tried to bury it beneath rumors and resistance.

WHY DID I REFUSED TO FAIL?

It would have been easy to lash out, to defend myself at every turn, to fight battles waged in backrooms and whispers. But I knew something they didn't: My work would speak louder than their words. I didn't seek applause, I sought results. I didn't crave validation, I demanded accountability. I didn't need their approval, I needed progress for students, for teachers, for communities.

Leadership isn't about popularity. True leadership means being comfortable with discomfort, knowing that progress will always be met with resistance. Not everyone will celebrate you. Not everyone will accept you. Some people will resent the change you represent. But I didn't come this far for them.

THE POWER OF PURPOSE OVER POLITICS

I lead for the students who need someone to fight for their future. I lead for the teachers who need direction, the communities that need revitalization, the schools that deserve better. I lead because leadership is about action, not titles.

I didn't quit. Every setback became fuel. Every failure became a lesson. And just like on the football field, I learned to adjust, to pivot, to push forward even when everything in me wanted to stop. My experiences in college weren't just about education, they were about resilience, about proving to myself and the world that I was more than a statistic, and more than a product of my environment.

LEADERSHIP IN ACTION: *How Football Prepared Me for Running a District*

Leadership, at its core, is about discipline, strategy, and execution, the same principles that made me successful on the football field. Running a district is no different than running a team. You must study the opposition, anticipate challenges, and execute with precision. Just like in football, success isn't about individual talent; it's about building a system where everyone plays their role to the best of their ability.

BUILDING A TEAM IS LIKE BUILDING A DEFENSE: *Trust, Discipline, and Execution*

A great leader isn't the one who does it all alone. It's the one who builds a team strong enough to withstand any challenge. I built my leadership team the same way I built my defense on the field:

Trust: Every player on a defense must trust the man next to him. If one person fails, the whole unit suffers. Leadership is no different. I surrounded myself with people who believed in the mission, who understood that we weren't just running a district, we were changing lives.

Discipline: There is no success without discipline. I instilled a culture where excellence wasn't optional, it was expected. Just like in football, there are no shortcuts in leadership. You put in the work, or you don't get the results.

Execution: It's not enough to have a plan you, must execute. Ideas without action are just dreams. I made sure my team didn't just talk about change; we delivered it. We reformed policies, built stronger student support systems, and ensured that every child, no matter their background, had a real shot at success.

INSTILLING A CULTURE OF EXCELLENCE AND EMPOWERMENT

In East St. Louis, I learned that mediocrity wasn't an option. If you weren't tenacious, if you weren't excellent, you got left behind. That mentality followed me into leadership. I didn't just want to lead; I wanted to build a culture where tenacity and excellence wasn't the exception but the standard.

That meant holding people accountable. That meant pushing students, staff, and even myself beyond what we thought was possible. That meant refusing to accept excuses and demanding results. But more importantly, it meant empowering others, showing them that, they too, had the ability to lead, rise, and break through barriers. And as long as I have breath in my body and a vision in my heart, I will keep leading, keep striving, and keep proving that character is defined not by words, but by results.

Chapter 8

CHANGING LIVES, ONE STUDENT AT A TIME

E ducation is not just about policies, curriculum, or standardized tests. It is about people, the students who walk into classrooms every day, carrying burdens unseen, struggles unspoken, and potential untapped. It is about recognizing that behind every statistic is a life, behind every challenge is a story, and behind every disengaged student is someone waiting to be reached. I know this because I have lived it. I was once that student. I had sat at those desks, walked those hallways, and fought against a system that didn't always seem built for me. That is what makes my leadership different. I do not lead from a distance. I lead from within, from a place of understanding, from a place of knowing what it truly takes to move students forward, not through force, but through belief, connection, and action.

THE STORIES THAT FUELED MY MISSION

Every student I encounter has a story. Some of them remind me of my own, while others reveal struggles I never had to endure. But the common thread is this: too many of them feel unseen, unheard, and unimportant.

I remember one student, let's call him Marcus. He was labeled a troublemaker, the kind of kid most teachers dreaded seeing on their roster. He had a reputation, not for his academic abilities, but for his disruptions, his defiance, his refusal to conform. But when I sat with him, when I peeled back the labels others had placed on him, I saw something else: a young man who had been failed too many times to believe in anything different.

Marcus wasn't a bad kid. He was a kid who had learned that survival meant pushing back before anyone could push him down. He had been written off so many times that he figured it was easier to live up to the expectations of failure than to fight against them. But I refused to let that be his story's ending. I spoke to him, not at him, but to him. I shared my story. I told him about the struggles I faced, the times I felt lost, the moments when, I too, wanted to give up. And for the first time, I saw something shift in his eyes: recognition.

That's the power of being one of them, of understanding, not in theory but in experience. When students see someone who has walked their path, who has faced their challenges and still emerged victorious, it gives them something invaluable: *hope*.

TURNING STRUGGLING SCHOOLS INTO PLACES OF SUCCESS

A school is more than a building; it is a battleground where futures are either won or lost. And too often, the schools that struggle the most are the ones left behind, underfunded, under-resourced, and underserved.

When I stepped into my role as a leader, I knew that changing these schools wouldn't be easy. But I was built for hard fights. I started by walking through the halls, sitting in the classrooms, and listening not just to the numbers but to the people. Speaking with teachers who had lost their passion because the system had drained them. I met students who had stopped trying because no one had ever told them they could succeed. I watched administrators struggle with outdated policies that did nothing but hold kids back. I knew that transformation wouldn't come from board meetings alone, it had to happen in the trenches. So, I rolled up my sleeves and got to work.

Redefining expectations: Too often, struggling schools are treated as if failure is inevitable. I changed that narrative. I told my staff, my students, and my community that success wasn't optional, it was expected.

Empowering teachers: A school is only as strong as its educators. I invested in my teachers, giving them the training, support, and resources they needed to truly teach, not just survive the day.

Creating student-first practices: I restructured disciplinary models to focus on restoration over punishment. Instead of pushing kids out, we found ways to bring them back in, to make them feel like they belonged.

And slowly, the tide began to turn.

The failing schools started producing graduates instead of dropouts. The kids labeled as "problems" started leading instead of disrupting. The teachers who had been burned out found their fire again. It wasn't magic. It was work, relentless, back-breaking, unapologetic work. But the work was working.

THE CHALLENGES OF EDUCATIONAL REFORM AND PUSHING PAST RESISTANCE

For every success, there was a fight. Educational reform is not welcomed with open arms. People cling to what they know, even if what they know is broken. There were pushbacks, battles, and opposition from people who were more comfortable with mediocrity than with change. Some parents didn't believe things could get better and resisted new approaches. Some educators were so used to the old system that they feared what change might bring. Some policymakers wanted results without wanting to invest in the hard work it took to get there. But I was not in this for easy wins. I was in this to change lives. So, I fought. I sat in meetings and demanded resources. I stood in front of boards and defended my students. I pushed against policies that treated kids like statistics instead of human beings. And yes, there were setbacks. There were moments when the resistance felt overwhelming as I questioned if the system was too rigid to break. But then, I would walk into a classroom and see a student who had once been failing, now thriving. I received a message from a young person who had once been counted out, now heading to college or starting a career. I started to see teachers regaining their love for education, knowing that they were part of something bigger than themselves. That is why I never stopped.

THE LEGACY OF ONE CHANGED LIFE

If there is one thing I have learned, it is this: changing one life can change everything. Because one life becomes a ripple. That student who was once on the verge of dropping out now believes in his future. When encouraged, they go on to succeed, to inspire their younger siblings, and to break generational cycles. That one teacher who rediscovers their passion goes on to inspire hundreds of students in their career. That one policy change that keeps kids in school instead of pushing them out creates opportunities where none existed before. I have seen firsthand how education can lift, transform, and resurrect. This journey has never been just about leading a district or reforming policies. It has always been about the students, the people, the stories. As long as there are students walking into schools with doubt in their eyes and untapped greatness in their hearts, my mission will continue. Because one changed life is never just one, it is the beginning of something greater.

Chapter 9

THE LEGACY OF A LEADER

When I reflect on my journey, from the halls of all my formal educational institutions to the communities and institutions where I've made an impact, I realize that leadership is not about personal accolades. It is about transformation. It is about ensuring that the footprints I leave are not just marks in the sand, but steppingstones for those who come after me.

Leadership is about people. It is about students who find confidence in their voices, teachers who regain their passion, and communities that evolve because someone took the time to care. The weight of this responsibility is not lost on me. I stand today as a leader not because of my own strength alone, but because of the many hands that once reached back to pull me forward.

FROM STRUGGLE TO STRENGTH: *The Journey Of Leadership*

Growing up in East St. Louis, Illinois, I learned resilience before I even understood the word. Life in my community was not designed for ease; it was built on survival. The schools I attended, the streets I walked, and the experiences I lived through, all painted a reality where success was not guaranteed, and opportunities were few and far between. But even in those circumstances, I saw leadership. I saw it in the teachers who stayed after school to ensure we understood our lessons, in the community leaders who fought for better resources, in the parents who worked tirelessly to provide for their families. These were my first examples of leadership, not in suits and boardrooms, but in the everyday acts of perseverance and sacrifice.

When I arrived at Lane College, I was met with a different kind of leadership, one that nurtured, challenged, and demanded growth. Pres. Chambers, Dean Thomas, Dr. Garcia, Mr./Mrs. Kirkendoll, Ms. Lovelady, were not just educators; they were architects of transformation. They saw potential in students like me and cultivated it. They held us accountable, pushed us to think bigger, and instilled a sense of responsibility to give back. This was where I learned that leadership was not just about personal success, but about creating pathways for others to rise.

IMPACTING STUDENTS: *A Duty, Not an Option*

I have always believed that true leadership is measured by the lives you change. One of the most defining aspects of my journey has been my work with students, young minds searching for direction, guidance, and someone who believes in them.

There was a student I will never forget. He was bright but burdened. Life had thrown challenges at him that no young person should have to endure. He was on the verge of giving up, convinced that his future had already been written. But leadership meant stepping into that moment, pulling him aside, and reminding him that his story was still his to write. I didn't just give him advice; I invested in him. I listened. I provided opportunities for growth. I connected him with resources and mentors who could guide him beyond what I alone could offer. Years later he returned not as a struggling student, but as a leader himself, mentoring others just as I had mentored him. That is legacy. That is what we call

IMPACT. My work with students extends beyond the classroom or counseling sessions. It is in the conversations held in hallways, the crisis interventions that change trajectories, and the advocacy that ensures they are seen and heard.

REVITALIZING EDUCATORS: *Re-igniting Passion*

It is not just students who need guidance, teachers too sometimes find themselves lost in the system, disillusioned by bureaucracy, and overwhelmed by the weight of their roles. I have witnessed firsthand how the fire that once burned in passionate educators can be dimmed by the realities of their profession.

Leadership in this space meant reigniting that passion. It meant reminding educators why they started in the first place. It meant creating professional development programs that were not just checkboxes, but truly transformative experiences. It meant advocating for their needs, ensuring that their voices were included in decision-making, and fostering a culture of collaboration. When a teacher finds purpose again, the ripple effect is undeniable. Classrooms become spaces of innovation and inspiration, students feel the shift in energy, and schools become places of possibility rather than obligation.

COMMUNITY LEADERSHIP: *Building Beyond the Classroom*

My role as a leader extends beyond students and teachers, it reaches into the heart of the community. Schools do not operate in isolation; they are a reflection of the communities they serve. If we want to change education, we must also invest in the environments that shape our students before they ever step into a classroom. This means working with community leaders, advocating for policy changes, creating mentorship programs, and ensuring that students have support beyond the school walls. It means being present, not just at meetings, but in neighborhoods, in homes, in spaces where real change happens. One of the most rewarding aspects of community leadership has been mentoring young professionals, those who aspire to lead but need guidance on how to navigate the challenges that come with it. Leadership is not about hoarding knowledge; it is about passing it down, ensuring that the next generation is equipped to carry the torch forward.

LEAVING A BLUEPRINT: *The Responsibility of Legacy*

What does it mean to leave a legacy? It means creating something that lasts beyond your presence. It means building structures that others can step into, refining systems so that those who follow do not have to struggle in the same ways. It means making your leadership replicable, ensuring that the lessons you've learned are not lost but, multiplied.

For me, legacy is not just about the students I've mentored or the educators I've empowered. It is about setting a standard of leadership, one rooted in service, integrity, humility and impact. It is about proving that where you start does not determine where you finish. It is about showing that leadership is not about titles or recognition, but about the lives you touch along the way.

As I move forward, I do so with the knowledge that my work is not done. There are still students to uplift, teachers to inspire, and communities to strengthen. That is the beauty of legacy, it is not an ending, but a continuation. And so, I press on, not just as a leader, but as a servant, knowing that the true measure of my success will be seen in the lives of those I've helped to rise.

Chapter 10
THE POWER OF ONE –
ANYONE CAN RISE

The world will tell you that you're just one person, that your voice doesn't matter, that your effort is too small to change anything. It's a lie. I know because I've lived it. I've seen what happens when one person decides to stand up, speak out, and push forward even when the odds are stacked high against them. I've seen the power of one, and I've watched it ripple outward, transforming lives, families, schools, and entire communities.

This chapter isn't just about my story, it's about your story. It's about reminding you that you have more power than you realize, and that no obstacle is insurmountable if you believe in yourself and put in the work. So, let's talk about rising, what it really takes to get up when life knocks you down and to keep climbing, one step at a time.

THE MOMENT THAT CHANGED EVERYTHING

I wasn't supposed to make it. Statistically, my story should have been one of struggle without triumph. I grew up in East St. Louis, a place where too many dreams were deferred, where too many people believed that success was something that happened to other people. But then, one day, someone saw me. It wasn't a grand moment. There were no fireworks, no movie-worthy speeches. It was just a mentor, someone who had walked the same uncertain path, who took the time to say, "I see something in you." That's the power of one. That one conversation planted a seed in me that grew into resilience. That one belief gave me permission to believe in myself. And that belief fueled every decision, every risk, every step that took me from where I was to where I am now. And here's what I learned: You don't need an entire army to change your life. You don't need the perfect circumstances, the perfect connections, or even the perfect plan. You just need to start.

FROM ONE TO MANY: *A Lesson From The Classroom*

Early in my career, I walked into a classroom full of chaos. A tough school, a tough crowd, and honestly, I wasn't sure I was going to make it through the day, let alone the year. The students had checked out before I even opened my mouth.

But then I noticed him. One student sitting in the back, doodling in his notebook. Something about him caught my attention, not because he was the loudest or the most disruptive, but because he was the most disconnected. I made a decision in that moment. If I could reach just one student that day, I'd call it a win. I walked over, crouched down by his desk, and asked, "What are you drawing?" He looked at me like I had two heads but showed me anyway, a detailed sketch of a superhero, muscles bulging, cape flying in the wind. "Who's that?" I asked. "It's me," he said quietly. "If I had powers."

In that moment, I saw the spark. And I realized that my job wasn't just to teach history or English, it was to remind these kids that they already had powers. They didn't need capes or super-strength. They had the power to rise, to change their story, to become whoever they wanted to be. That one conversation led to another, and another. Slowly but surely, that student started engaging. He started believing in himself.

And as he rose, others followed. By the end of the year, that classroom wasn't the same place it had been on day one. All because of one small moment, one small effort that turned into something much bigger.

THE POWER OF ONE: *Breaking It Down*

So, what does it mean to harness the power of one? It means recognizing that every action you take, no matter how small, can have an impact. It means understanding that you don't have to wait for someone else to make a change, you can be the change. Here's how:

1. Own Your Story

Your past doesn't define your future, but it's part of your story and owning it is the first step to rising. I've faced plenty of obstacles, from growing up in a challenging environment to navigating the difficulties of higher education and leadership. But I never let those challenges define me. Instead, I used them as fuel to push harder, aim higher, and prove to myself that I could overcome anything.

Ask yourself: What's holding you back? What story are you telling yourself about who you are and what you're capable of? If it's a story of limitations, it's time to rewrite it.

2. Take One Step at a Time

Rising doesn't happen overnight. It's a process, and it starts with one step. Maybe that step is going back to school, applying for a job, starting a business, or simply getting out of bed and facing the day. Whatever it is, take it, and then take another, and another. Momentum builds quickly when you keep moving forward.

3. Find Your Why

What drives you? What keeps you going when things get tough? For me, it's always been about giving back, about making sure that the people I lead, mentor, and teach have the tools they need to succeed. Your "why" might be different, but it's just as important. When you know what you're fighting for, it's easier to stay the course.

4. Lift Others as You Rise

This is the real secret to the power of one: It multiplies when you share it. Every time you mentor someone, encourage someone, or help someone rise; you're creating a ripple effect that can change the world. Don't just focus on your own success, use your journey to inspire and empower others.

ONE PERSON, ONE DECISION, ONE LEGACY

There's a young woman I mentored years ago who had every reason to give up. Life had been cruel to her. She had been told no, more times than she could count. She had every excuse to walk away from her dreams. But one day, she decided to fight. She applied for one more opportunity, even though the last ten hadn't worked out. She knocked on one more door, even though so many had been slammed in her face. That one choice led to an acceptance letter. That acceptance letter led to a degree. That degree led to a career that changed not only her life, but the lives of her family and community all because of one decision.

WHAT'S YOUR ONE?

Maybe your one decision is to finally believe in yourself. Maybe it's to forgive yourself for past mistakes. Maybe it's to reach out to a mentor, to start a project, to take a risk you've been too afraid to take. Whatever it is, do it. The world changes when one person decides to rise.

You might be just one person, but that's all it takes to change the world. And if changing the world that we all live in is too big for you at this moment and time, then try making a difference in the world that you live in.

Chapter 11

FINAL PLAY – WRITING YOUR OWN STORY

Life is not a spectator sport. You don't get to sit on the sidelines, waiting for someone to hand you the perfect opportunity, the perfect moment, the perfect life. If you want to win, you must step onto the field. You must take the final play into your own hands.

This chapter is about that moment, the moment where you decide whether you will keep letting life happen to you, or if you will take charge and start writing your own story.

I've met too many people who believe their story is already written, as if where they were born, what they've been through, or what mistakes they've made somehow determine their final destination. But let me tell you something: you hold the pen. You get to decide what happens next. And if you think the odds are too stacked against you, trust me, I've been there. I'm here to tell you: Success is not about where you start. It's about where you're willing to go.

BREAKING FREE FROM THE SCRIPT YOU DIDN'T WRITE

For years, I let other people's expectations shape the way I saw myself. Growing up in East St. Louis, I was told what was possible for someone like me and it wasn't much. The script had already been written; struggle, mediocrity, and settling for less than my potential. But one day, I realized something:

just because someone hands you a script doesn't mean you have to follow it.

Maybe you've been told that you're not smart enough, not talented enough, not lucky enough. Maybe life has beaten you down so many times that you've started to believe that this is just the way things are. But hear me when I say this: your past is not your prison, and your circumstances are not your destiny. The moment you decide to take control of your future is the moment your life starts to change.

YOUR FUTURE IS NOT ON AUTOPILOT, TAKE THE WHEEL

One of the biggest mistakes people make is assuming that life will just "work itself out." It won't. You can't just drift through life and expect to land somewhere great. If you don't take control of where you're going, life will take control for you, and it rarely leads to the place you want to be. Think about it: The most successful people in the world didn't get there by accident. They had a vision. They made a plan. They made choices, sometimes hard ones, that took them from where they were to where they wanted to be. The same is true for you.

So, here's your challenge: Stop waiting. Stop hesitating. Stop thinking you need permission to chase your dreams. The only person who can truly hold you back is you. Success is a journey, not a straight line. Let's be real, taking control of your life doesn't mean everything will suddenly become easy. You're going to fail. You're going to doubt yourself. You're going to have moments where you wonder if it's even worth it. That's part of the process. Success isn't about never falling; it's about getting back up every single time you do. Every obstacle, every setback, every rejection is all part of the story. It's all fuel for the next chapter.

I remember one of the hardest setbacks I ever faced. I had worked for years to reach a leadership position, only to be told that I wasn't "the right fit." After all the work, the sacrifices, the long nights it felt like everything had been for nothing. I had a choice to make, I could let that moment define me, or I could use it as fuel to push even harder. I chose the latter. And because I refused to give up, I did reach my goal, not in that place, but in a better one, on my own terms. Your setbacks do not define your success. Your response to them does.

NEVER FORGET WHERE YOU CAME FROM, BUT DON'T LET IT LIMIT YOU

There's a fine balance in life between honoring your past and being trapped by it. I carry East St. Louis with me everywhere I go. The lessons, the struggles, the people who shaped me, they are part of my foundation. But I also knew that my hometown didn't define my limits. I didn't have to stay in the same place, repeat the same patterns, or accept the same circumstances. The same is true for you. Where you come from is important. Your experiences are important. But don't ever let them put a ceiling on your potential. You can honor your roots while still reaching for something bigger. And when you do succeed, when you break through, remember to turn around and pull others up with you. That's what real success looks like, not just elevating yourself, but creating opportunities for others to rise, too.

THE FINAL PLAY: *It's Your Move*

Every game comes down to a final play. The question is, are you going to take the shot?

You have two choices:

1. You can keep sitting on the sidelines, playing it safe, and letting life happen to you.

2. Or you can grab the pen, step onto the field, and start writing about the life you want to live.

This is your final play, your defining moment, your chance to stop letting the world tell you who you are and start deciding for yourself. So, what's your next move? Because I promise you this: The only way to lose is to never try. Now go write your own damn story.

EPILOGUE: *A Life Still in Motion*

If you think the story ends here, you're mistaken. The credits haven't rolled. The book hasn't closed. My journey, just like yours, is still in motion. Every chapter I've written so far, every lesson I've learned, every battle I've fought and won (and even the ones I lost) have all led to this moment. And if there's one thing I know for certain, it's this: I'm not done yet.

The truth is, real leaders, real dreamers, real game-changers never stop evolving. They never stop pushing, growing, and reaching for the next level. That's exactly where I find myself now, on the edge of my next great chapter. This is not the end. It's a launchpad.

THE NEXT CHAPTER: *Building, Mentoring, and Leaving a Legacy*

As I look forward, my mission has never been clearer. Every lesson I've learned along the way has prepared me for this next phase of my journey, one centered around entrepreneurship, mentorship, and creating something that will outlive me. I've always believed that the real measure of success isn't just how far you go, it's how many people you bring with you. That's why mentorship has been, and will continue to be, a pillar of my life's work. I've walked the path of uncertainty. I've faced self-doubt, the closed doors, and the uphill battles. And now, I have a responsibility to reach back and pull others forward, to give them the roadmap I had to figure out for myself.

There are young professionals out there right now who have all the talent, all the potential, but they lack guidance. They lack the right connections. They lack someone to look at them and say, "I see something in you." I intend to be that someone. But mentorship isn't just about words, it's about creating opportunities. And that's where entrepreneurship comes in.

FROM STUDENT TO TEACHER, FROM EMPLOYEE TO OWNER

For years, I played by the rules. I climbed the ladder. I worked the undesired jobs. I put in the time. But now, I've reached the point where I'm ready to take ownership, not just of my career, but of my impact. Entrepreneurship isn't just about financial freedom or business success. It's about building something that matters. It's about creating something that doesn't just serve me, but serves my community.

I'm stepping into this next chapter knowing that every business venture, every leadership initiative, every move I make isn't just for me, it's for the next generation watching, learning, and preparing to take their own leap. Because here's the reality: Ownership is power. And too many people, especially those who come from backgrounds like mine, have been conditioned to believe that they must wait for someone else to give them a chance. No more. It's time to start creating our own chances.

THE WORK NEVER STOPS AND THAT'S A GOOD THING

Some people chase an endpoint. They want to "arrive." They want to check off all the boxes and say, I made it. But I don't believe in that. I believe in motion. I believe in constant evolution. I believe in never getting too comfortable. Because the second you stop moving, the second you stop growing, you start fading. And I didn't come this far to fade. The work of leading, mentoring, and uplifting doesn't stop just because you've hit a certain level of success. If anything, the higher you climb, the greater your responsibility to those coming behind you.

So, as I step into this next phase, as a business owner, as a mentor, as a leader who refuses to slow down, I do so with the understanding that my purpose is bigger than me. And if you've been following this journey, if you've taken anything from these pages, let this be your takeaway: You are never done. Keep moving. Keep building. Keep creating. Keep learning. Keep giving back. Because the moment you think you've "made it" is the moment you stop making a difference. I'm still in motion. And if you've been inspired by this journey, I challenge you to stay in motion too. There's still more to do. So, let's get to work.

SILENT STRENGHT: LESSONS FROM EAST ST. LOUIS

There is a misconception people have about leadership, that it belongs to the loudest voice in the room, the most charismatic speaker, the one who dominates conversations and commands attention with sheer force. But long before I held any formal title, East St. Louis taught me a different definition of leadership, one rooted in quiet power, action over words, and the ability to move without the need for fanfare.

Growing up in East St. Louis, I wasn't the one walking around trying to make a name for myself by talking big. I wasn't the kind to puff up my chest or make empty threats to look tough. I learned early that words are wind, they stir the air, but don't move the earth. In a city where survival was often based on how you carried yourself; I found power in silence. I learned to let others bark while I studied, calculated, and waited for the right moment to move. It wasn't because I was passive. It was because I understood that words alone couldn't save you when the real tests came. I wasn't looking for applause or validation. I didn't need witnesses to see how I moved. If you crossed a line with me, I wouldn't meet you in the court of public opinion, I'd settle things directly, without a crowd, without noise.

Those streets taught me that leadership, at its core, is about knowing when to act and when to hold back. It's about mastering your emotions and letting action speak in spaces where words lose their power. I remember one particular day standing outside a corner store watching a guy try to bait me in front of a few familiar faces. He wanted a show. He wanted to prove something at my expense. But what he didn't understand was that I'd never been the type to give people the drama they craved. I gave him nothing in the moment, no reaction, no argument, just a steady stare that promised a different kind of conversation later. And when that conversation came, there were no witnesses just me, him, and clarity. I carried that same principle with me far beyond East St. Louis into classrooms, boardrooms, and leadership circles. As I climbed into roles where people expected me to lead hundreds, even thousands, I realized those street lessons were more relevant than ever.

In leadership, people will test you. They will poke, prod, and sometimes try to undermine you in front of others, hoping to get a rise. What I learned back home was this: If you react impulsively to every challenge, you give away your power. If you waste energy on proving yourself in every meeting, you dilute your authority. Instead, I chose to lead with the quiet strength I developed on those streets.

In boardrooms, I never felt the need to dominate conversations to be respected. I let others speak, I listened, and when I finally spoke, people paid attention, not because I was loud, but because I was measured. And when tough decisions needed to be made, I made them decisively, without theatrics or indecision.

THE STREET CODE THAT SHAPED MY LEADERSHIP

I still apply the same unspoken rules I lived by in East St. Louis to how I lead organizations:

- ➤ Stay calm under pressure. When tension rises, I don't match it with panic. I move with composure, the same way I did when situations or when the block got heated. Leaders set the emotional tone.
- ➤ Avoid unnecessary battles. Just like back home, not every challenge requires a public fight. I've learned to pick my battles and handle many situations quietly behind the scenes. The most effective moves are often the ones no one sees.
- ➤ Don't bluff. Mean what you say. I don't make idle threats, and I don't make promises I can't keep. If I tell a staff member or a partner that something will happen, it will happen. People respect leaders who stand on their word, not those who posture.
- ➤ Presence over noise. My demeanor, like back in East St. Louis, still speaks louder than my voice. I don't

need to "perform leadership" to be effective. I've built a reputation for consistency and action, not grandstanding.

These aren't just survival tactics; they are leadership strategies rooted in my identity and my story. What East St. Louis gave me wasn't just toughness. It gave me discipline, emotional intelligence, and the ability to navigate adversity with a calm head and steady hands. And while I traded street corners for boardrooms and school campuses, the fundamentals haven't changed. The biggest myth people believe is that you must be loud to be heard. I've learned that the strongest leaders don't need to raise their voices; they just need to move with certainty. Because when you come from a place where every step could mean survival or failure, you learn to move deliberately and that's what leadership is about.

Deliberate steps. Thoughtful actions. Quiet strength.

MY SPIRITUAL UPBRINGING

Every day in East St. brought its own set of challenges, I learned that survival wasn't just about physical endurance, it was also about spiritual resilience. The adversity, the trials, and the setbacks could have easily consumed me, but it was my mother and my unwavering faith in God that carried me through. In addition to my mother, another one of my greatest sources of strength has always been the book of Job. Job's story, a man who lost everything yet never wavered in his trust in God, always seemed to resonate deeply with me. Like Job, I experienced seasons of hardship, where it felt as if everything, I worked for was stripped away. Yet, like him, I learned that faith is forged in fire.

There were moments when the struggle seemed unbearable, times when I questioned the purpose behind the pain. But prayer became my lifeline, and belief became my anchor. My faith reminded me that there was a greater plan, even when I couldn't see it. Without that faith, without the constant conversations with God and the ability to draw from the spiritual lessons I learned, I know this journey would have stopped long before reaching the seat of the superintendency.

The journey "From the Ashes of Struggle to the Seat of Superintendency" is more than a professional achievement; it's a testament to divine grace and endurance. It's proof that faith, when coupled with perseverance, can carry you from the depths of despair to the heights of leadership. I am fully aware that I did not walk this path alone. Every promotion, every breakthrough, every hard-fought victory was God's hand at work, guiding me, shaping me, and preparing me to lead others.

CONCLUSION
Forged in Fire: How East St. Louis Shaped My
Journey to Educational Leadership

I WAS NOT SUPPOSED TO MAKE IT THIS FAR.

Growing up in East St. Louis, I saw dreams deferred, potential squandered, and bright futures dimmed by circumstance. The world around me was a battleground, one where poverty, violence, and systemic neglect loomed often. But in that same space, I also witnessed resilience, strength, and a resolute will to survive. I was raised in a city that demanded toughness, where nothing was given, and everything had to be earned. It was there, in the heart of struggle, that I found my purpose.

I learned earlier that if I wanted something, I had to fight for it. I had to work twice as hard, be twice as prepared, and refuse to let my surroundings dictate my destiny. I saw too many young people, full of promise, fall through the cracks. I refused to be one of them. My community, my family, and my own experiences instilled a fire in me, one that would not be extinguished, no matter how many obstacles stood in my way.

BECOMING THE MENTOR, I ONCE NEEDED

That fire led me to education, first as a teacher. I understood my students because I had lived their reality. I walked through school doors carrying the weight of things I couldn't control, feeling the unspoken expectations, some from those who believed in me, and some from those who had already written me off. So, when I stood in front of my classroom, I did more than teach, I saw my students. I saw

121

their fears, their struggles, and their dreams. I knew that for many of them, school was not just a place of learning; it was their only refuge, their only chance at something greater.

Teaching wasn't enough. I wanted to do more. I wanted to break cycles, to reach the students who were slipping through the cracks. That's what led me to social work. I wasn't content with just delivering lessons, I wanted to understand the deeper issues, the struggles that happened outside the classroom. I became an advocate, fighting for the resources and opportunities that so many children in underserved communities never received. I sat with families who had lost hope, listened to students whose voices had been silenced, and worked to build bridges between education and the community.

CLIMBING THE LADDER, CARRYING MY PEOPLE WITH ME *(The Entire City of East Saint)*

Every step of my career was driven by something greater than ambition. I did not climb the ladder for prestige, I climbed so I could lift others as I rose. As an assistant principal, then a principal, I didn't just manage schools; I transformed them. I led with the urgency of someone who knew what was at stake. I pushed for higher expectations, for equity, for real change. I refused to accept the idea that some children, particularly Black and Brown children in struggling districts, were destined for less. I challenged systems that had been built to keep them stagnant.

That same fire carried me into district leadership, first in St. Louis Public Schools, then in Riverview Gardens, Olathe, and Normandy. I knew that if I wanted to make a real, lasting change, I had to be at the decision-making table. I had to be where policies were shaped, where resources were distributed and futures were determined. I fought for the underdogs, for the students who reminded me of myself. I carried the weight of every child who had ever been told they weren't good enough, every teacher who had ever been undervalued, and every community that had ever been left behind. I led with urgency, with passion, and with the understanding that education is not just about books, it is about survival, opportunity, and freedom.

DIFFICULTY: *The Fabric of My Existence*

Difficulty is a word that most fear, a reality many seek to escape, and a force that has broken the unprepared and the unwilling. For me, however, difficulty is not an enemy, nor is it a foreign concept. It is the foundation upon which I was built, the forge in which my resilience was tempered, and the battlefield upon which I have proven my worth time and time again. Difficulty is not new to me; it is as familiar as my own reflection, as constant as the air I breathe. I do not shrink in the face of adversity, I thrive in it. Every fiber of my being was crafted in the fires of hardship, and I have learned not just to survive but to dominate within the storm.

BORN INTO THE CRUCIBLE

I entered this world not with the luxury of ease, but with the weight of struggle pressing upon my newborn chest. From my first breath, difficulty sat at my bedside, whispering the hard truths of the world into my infant ears. I was born in a city that did not make success a gift but, a conquest where every step forward was a battle, and every dream was a fortress that had to be taken by force. East St. Louis, a place known for its unyielding streets and its ability to either crush or carve out warriors, was my birthplace and my training ground.

I did not grow up shielded from the world's sharp edges. I grew up feeling their cut, learning their angles, and mastering how to move through them without flinching. While some were coddled in the arms of comfort, I was sharpened by the hands of hardship.

The lessons came early: trust was earned, not given; strength was not just physical but mental; and failure was not an end, but a sharpening stone for future victories.

THE ART OF STRUGGLE

Many see struggle as something to escape from, but for me, struggle is where I perform at my best. Some people freeze in difficult situations, but I come alive. There is something about the pressure, the urgency, the weight of challenge pressing down that brings out my sharpest instincts and my most calculated decisions. The streets of my youth were not paved with opportunity, but I learned to carve my own path where none existed. I learned to fight battles not just with my fists but with my mind, knowing that brute strength alone would never be enough to escape the gravity of my circumstances.

Education had become my weapon of choice. I knew that if I wanted to command my own destiny, I had to arm myself with knowledge. While many around me were content to let their environment dictate their fate, I saw difficulty as an invitation to rise higher. I didn't just want to survive; I wanted to master the very forces that sought to keep me down. So, I studied, I worked, I strategized. I collected degrees not as trophies but as weapons, each one sharpening me further, making me more formidable.

MASTERING THE BATTLEFIELD

Life has thrown me challenges that would have left others broken, but I have always met them head-on. When doors were closed, I built my own. When obstacles were placed in my path, I turned them into steppingstones. Whether it was breaking barriers in education, rising through the ranks in leadership, or pushing through the weight of expectations, I have never backed down.

Difficult situations do not intimidate me; they excite me. Where others see a dead end, I see an opportunity to push harder, think smarter, and maneuver faster. Some people pray for an easy road, I have never needed one. I do not fear difficulty because I understand it, I respect it, and above all, I owned it.

DIFFICULTY IS MY BACKYARD

At the end of the day, difficulty is not some distant storm that comes and goes in my life. It is not a seasonal visitor or a temporary inconvenience. Difficulty is my backyard, it is the place I know best, the space where I am most comfortable, and the terrain where I move with confidence. I do not run from the struggle because the struggle is where I was made.

Others may wilt in the face of hardship, but I stand firm because I have never known another way. Adversity is not my enemy, it is my oldest teacher, my toughest coach, and my most reliable companion. Some people are born into privilege, but I was born into battle. And from that battle, I emerged not just stronger but unstoppable.

Difficulty does not define me, it fuels me. While others may get lost in their comfort zones, I navigate the rough terrain with ease. Because at the end of the day, difficulty is not just where I came from, it is where I belong.

REFUSING TO BE DENIED

But I knew that experience alone would not be enough. The world does not always respect passion, it respects credentials. And so, I made myself undeniable. I earned a Bachelor of Science, a Master of Social Work, a Master of Business Administration, a Master of Educational Administration, and a Doctorate in Educational Leadership. Not because I wanted titles, but because I wanted power, the power to change lives, to disrupt failing systems, to be in spaces where people who came from where I came from were often excluded. I studied relentlessly, knowing that every degree, every certification, every milestone was a weapon in my arsenal. I was building something bigger than myself. I was proving that a child from East St. Louis could rise, not just to escape, but to return and lead.

A LEGACY OF IMPACT

I am not just an educator. I am a fighter. I am a builder. I am a product of East St. Louis, a city that did not break me, but built me. My past did not make me bitter; it made me unstoppable. It gave me the grit to stand in rooms where I was not always welcome, to make decisions that were not always easy, and to push for changes that were long overdue. It taught me that leadership is not about titles, it is about impact. And my impact will not be measured by the positions I've held, but by the lives I've touched, the doors I've opened, and the futures I've helped shape. Because I am not just a survivor of East St. Louis. I am a product of its strength. And that strength will continue to change the world.

A Special Message to You, Zenobia Charlotte Agnew (RIP)

Growing up in East St. Louis, a city known for its challenges and resilience, I often found myself navigating trials that tested my character, perseverance, and decision-making. Amid those struggles, one question consistently echoed in my mind: **If I did this, would my mom be proud?** That simple yet powerful question became a moral compass, influencing my actions, choices, and ultimately, my journey toward success.

My mother was a figure of strength and wisdom, embodying the kind of fortitude that was required to not only survive, but thrive in an environment where opportunities were scarce, and obstacles were many. Her sacrifices and unwavering commitment to family taught me that life's difficulties weren't excuses to give up, but challenges to overcome. I knew that every decision I made reflected not just on me but also on the values she instilled in me. Asking myself whether my choices would make her proud forced me to pause, reflect, and aim higher, even when circumstances tempted me to settle or take the easy route.

East St. Louis was a place where resilience was both a necessity and an art. Maneuvering through its challenges required more than brute strength, it demanded strategic thinking, adaptability, and a relentless will to push forward. The streets were unforgiving, but they also taught me valuable lessons: how to stand firm in the face of adversity, how to adapt when situations change, and how to overcome obstacles that seemed insurmountable. However, it was the constant internal dialogue; Would my mom approve of this? That kept me grounded and focused on a greater purpose.

This mindset didn't just shape my choices; it shaped who I became. It pushed me to strive for excellence in education, knowing that each diploma I earned wasn't just a piece of paper, but a testament to my ability to rise above my circumstances. It motivated me to embrace leadership roles, first as a teacher, then as a principal, and eventually as a superintendent, because I knew that these roles allowed me to honor her legacy by giving back and lifting others. It drove me to pursue multiple advanced degrees, not just to build my résumé, but because I understood that knowledge and expertise would open doors not just for me, but for the communities I served.

The trials I faced; poverty, systemic barriers, and the daily challenges of growing up in a city that often made headlines for the wrong reasons, could have easily defined me. But instead, they became the fire that forged my resolve. The question of my mom's pride reminded me that success wasn't just about personal achievements; it was about character, integrity, and the legacy I would leave behind. It kept me focused on the bigger picture: creating a life that honored her sacrifices and made her belief in me worthwhile.

Even now, as I look back on my journey and the milestones I've achieved, that question remains at the core of who I am. It's a reminder that my success wasn't accidental, it was driven by a deep desire to make her proud, to rise above the trials of my youth, and to create a legacy that reflects the values she instilled in me. Her influence and that guiding question didn't just drive me to succeed, they taught me to lead with purpose, humility, and a relentless commitment to excellence.

**My Mother was the epitome of
The Power Of One.**

THANK YOU, MOMMA

88cc5979-e757-42d7-b546-1fb8f70ae312R01